גימטריה

ג 3 י 10 מ 40 ט 9 ר 200 י 10 ה 5 = 277

Hebrew Letters Equal Numbers

עזר

ט 70 ז 7 ר 200 = 277

Means Help or Helper

GEMATRIA AZER

A Taste Of Torah From Genesis

Dr. Akiva Gamliel Belk

Dean of Jewish Studies at

B'nai Noach Torah Institute, LLC

ISBN-10: 0615952569

ISBN -13: 978-0615952567

Publisher

B'nai Noach Torah Institute, LLC,

Post Office Box 14

Cedar Hill, Missouri 63016

First Edition 2014

DEDICATED

To those desiring Ha Torah to Learn
Who feel the task of Ha Torah
too great to discern
Who think it may take forever to Learn
May I calm your concern?

Seek out a good Torah Teacher
Whose love and devotion to God
is his best feature
Whose desire to help others learn
makes that one a special Teacher
Whose study habits are another quality feature

Then cry out to the Creator with all your Heart
Then study study Ha Torah with
your entire being with every part
Then continue day after day until
Ha Torah has filled your heart.
Then humbly look back to your start...

FORWARD

Writing a book is a gargantuan project. I know!! My husband, Dr. Akiva Gamliel has written more than a dozen books. He has a real passion for sharing what he has learned. Writing with inspiration is a special gift Akiva has. Many nights my husband is awakened from his sleep by the Creator of the Universe. He softly says as he arises, 'I can't sleep. I need to study for awhile.' He then arises to study and record inspirations from our Creator, not wanting to miss any part of these revelations. He will write for hours.

Our Creator Enlightens Gematrias and other information during these times. The insights are new to us. Akiva does not consider himself special. He is a willing receptacle. When the Creator wants knowledge disseminated He can use any willing vessel. In our prayers we say, '...He who removes sleep from our eyelids...' There are many dedicated individuals our

Creator uses. There could me more if we were willing to give up our nights, our sleep, and things important to us just for Torah study! Dr. Akiva Gamliel Belk writes for hours at a time oblivious to whatever else is going on around him.

I have read all of my husbands books and have found each of them to be filled with great Torah insights and wisdom. This book, *Gematria Aizer, A Taste of Torah from Genesis* is a springboard to Torah Study and is easily understood. One can go to any depth they want in utilizing this Torah Study tool.

Studying with Akiva is an adventure. One never knows what thrill is around the next curve or what exciting point he is building up to until you are there.

Revi Belk
Dean of Ladies Studies
B'nai Noach Torah Institute, LLC

PREFACE

It very important to write a book that can fill hearts with Ha Torah and that can lend a hand in improving our relationship with The Lord God. Ha Torah is alive for all to learn, follow and enjoyed. Only Ha Torah has the power restore the weak and damaged parts of our lives . My goal and joy in writing this book was simply to share lessons from Gematria that are exciting to know while at the same time offer a few Words to lift and encourage our souls. Can there be a better reward? We wanted to reduce many of the formalities which precede a book to help keep the cost down. There is a brief introduction for each Parshat at the beginning of each Chapter. The glossary is woven into each individual page.

ACKNOWLEDGMENTS

Oh Creator of the Universe, thank You for this opportunity to share the Gematrias in this book. Thank You for forgiving us of our every sin. Thank You for helping us to return to Torah Observances. Thank You for daily assisting us with efforts to improve. Thank You for every blessing. Thank you for the bread of life. Thank you for Revi... Kaw Naw Nah Haw Raw.

My wife, Revi is a soft spoken, quite, tiny lady, in physical stature, but very big in showing others love, kindness, patience and Observing Torah Mitzvot. I love you Revi and thank our Creator for every breath He Has Given Us! Kaw Naw Nah Haw Raw. Revi thank you for assisting greatly with the editing and formatting of this book. I greatly appreciate your every effort!

Table of Contents

DEDICATED....................5
FORWARD....................7
PREFACE....................9
ACKNOWLEDGMENTS....................11
Vezot Ha Brachah....................15
Deuteronomy 33.1 - 34.12....................15
Bereisheit Bereisheit....................19
Genesis 1.1 - 6.8....................19
Bereisheit Noach....................27
Genesis 6.9 - 11.32....................27
Bereisheit Lech Lecha....................33
Genesis 12.1 - 17.27....................33
Bereisheit Vayera....................39
Genesis 18.1 - 22.24....................39
Bereisheit Chayei Sarah....................45
Genesis 23.1 - 25.18....................45
Bereisheit Toldot....................59
Genesis 25.19 - 28.9....................59
Bereisheit Vayeitzei....................71
Genesis 28.10 - 32.3....................71
Bereisheit Vayishlach....................81
Genesis 32.4 - - 36.43....................81
Bereisheit Vayeishev....................91

Genesis 37.1 - 40.22....................................91
Mikeitz..107
Genesis 41.1 - 44.17..................................107
Vayigash..119
Genesis 44.18 - 47.27................................119
Vayechi..127
Genesis 47.28 - 50.26................................127
GEMATRIA CHART.....................................133
Scripture Index..134
Gematria's...137
About The Author......................................138
Books By Dr. Akiva Gamliel.........................141

Vezot Ha Brachah

Deuteronomy 33.1 - 34.12

Which is the last of the Five Books of Ha Torah?

Which Chapter is the last Chapter in Ha Torah?

What Passuk / Verse
is the last Verse in Ha Torah?

What are the last three Words in Ha Torah?

What is the significance?

Every Word of Ha Torah is important. Each of us are important. We are at the time of the year when one Torah Cycle concludes and a new Torah Cycle begins God Willing. We are beginning this year's Torah Cycle Study with the completion of the last study from the previous year.

Devarim 34.12

וּלְכֹל הַיָּד הַחֲזָקָה וּלְכֹל הַמּוֹרָא הַגָּדוֹל אֲשֶׁר עָשָׂה
מֹשֶׁה לְעֵינֵי כָּל־יִשְׂרָאֵל

Deuteronomy 34.12

And in all that mighty hand, and in all the great and awesome deeds which Moses performed For the sight of all Israel.

Gematria

לְעֵינֵי כָּל־יִשְׂרָאֵל

For the sight of all Israel

170 = 10 י 50 נ 10 י 70 ע 30 ל

591 = 30 ל 1 א 200 ר 300 ש 10 י   30 ל 20 כ

761 = 170 + 591

וְנִשְׁתֶּה

Vih Neesh Teh / that we may drink

761 = 5 ה 400 ת 300 ש 50 נ 6 ו

לְעֵינֵי כָּל־יִשְׂרָאֵל Lih Ay Nay - Cawl Yisroel are the last three Words of Ha Torah. They are very significant as each Word of Ha Torah is. Notice that we are discussing sight. 'For all the sight of

Yisroel.' Our Creator Performed many miracles in Egypt and in the dessert for all Yisroel to see. Our Creator is going to perform many miracles in the future for all Yisroel to see. Now the Gematria of 761 Mystically instructs us to drink in these Miracles. Our Creator wants us to taste these miracles around our Sabbath Table and our High Holy Day table just as we taste Challah and Drink Wine. They are for our benefit.

Note the usage of the Words כָּל־יִשְׂרָאֵל. This is very important. It is important for what it Says and for what it does not say. It does not Say בְּנֵי־יִשְׂרָאֵל. It does not Say the twelve sons of Yaakov and his Descendants. It Says Kal Yisroel, meaning 'All Yisroel'. This is very significant because the Word כָּל is more inclusive. This means that any one living right here and now could be included. Those who are Jewish are included and those who are not Jewish may be included if at some point they were to convert to Judaism. God is Saying that the Miracles He performed were potentially for everyone. Those living then and those living in the future.

Bereisheit Bereisheit

Genesis 1.1 - 6.8

This is the first Parshat of twelve within the book of Genesis. Bereisheit means beginnings. When Bereisheit is repeated its '*Great beginnings*'.

Bereisheit 1.1 - 4

What Is The Creator's Revealed Light?

We live in a world that is bereft of Light, i.e. Spiritual light. The absence of Spiritual Light that guides our path that lights our way that causes us to care about what is going on around us is very obvious. A true Spiritual awareness causes us to be careful with how we speak with others. A lack of Spiritual Presence is evident with our immodest dress. The Spirituality that lit the path of political ethics is dark. Political language is full of lies and deceit!! Fair just business principles are waning. It is so dark that in some ways it is almost like we are at the beginning of time when our Creator Said, 'Let there be Light,' i.e. 'Let My Light [Ha Torah] be revealed.'

Bereisheit 1.1-4

בְּרֵאשִׁית בָּרָא אֱלֹהִים אֵת הַשָּׁמַיִם וְאֵת הָאָרֶץ׃ וְהָאָרֶץ
הָיְתָה תֹהוּ וָבֹהוּ וְחֹשֶׁךְ עַל־פְּנֵי תְהוֹם וְרוּחַ אֱלֹהִים
מְרַחֶפֶת עַל־פְּנֵי הַמָּיִם׃ וַיֹּאמֶר אֱלֹהִים יְהִי־אוֹר וַיְהִי־
אוֹר׃ וַיַּרְא אֱלֹהִים **אֶת־הָאוֹר** כִּי־טוֹב וַיַּבְדֵּל אֱלֹהִים בֵּין
הָאוֹר וּבֵין הַחֹשֶׁךְ׃

Genesis 1.1-4

In the beginning God Created everything from the Letter Aleph to the Letter Tav of the heavens and everything from the Letter Aleph to the Letter Tav of the earth. And the earth was without form, and void; and darkness was upon the face of the deep. And a wind from God Moved upon the face of the waters. And God Said, ***Let everything from the Letter Aleph to the Letter Tav of [My] Light; [be revealed] and there was Light.*** *And God Saw the Light, that it was good; and God divided the Light from the Darkness.*

This is the first four Verses of Ha Torah.

The Jewish understanding of the Ten Utterances in Creation mentioned in Pirkei Avot 5.1.

1. In the Beginning God Created the Heavens and the Earth. In other Words:

God Said, *Let there be Heavens and Earth,* - Genesis 1.1.

2. The Ruach... The Spirit of God hovered on the face of the waters. In other Words:

God Said... God Spoke... *God Breathed and the waters moved*, - Genesis 1.2.

3. God Said, *Let My Light be Revealed and there was the Light [of the Torah... the 613 Commands of the Torah]*, Genesis 1.3. In the Original Text the Words אֶת־הָאוֹר Eht - Ha - Ohr have a very strong mystical meaning. 'this includes everything from the first Letter of the Aleph Bet, the Aleph to the last Letter of the Aleph Bet, the Tav of the REVEALED Light. The Light... the Illumination

came from God. It is true that the Light the Illumination are Words. However these Words of Illumination are written. They are the 613 Commands written in the Torah. The Original language is Mystical in that each Letter has a numerical value. The Numerical value for Eht - Ha Ohr is 613. The 613 is representative of the 613 Commands God wrote in Ha Torah.

The enlightenment we receive flows from The Torah. We talk about the order of the Letter and how they point to God as First and only source of enlightenment.

We explain that the Words אֶת־הָאוֹר Eht Ha Ohr mean more than *everything from the Letter Aleph to the Letter Tav.* They speak of the method by which God Revealed His Light through the Torah. Eht Ha Ohr is the Gematria of 613. In The Torah God Reveals 613 Commands that all Creation is to follow. The textbook discusses this in greater detail. All the Bible flows from the 613 Commands of the Torah. Nothing exists without The Torah. The 613 Commands tells us what God Wants from us. They tell us what our

Creator Expects.

אֶת־הָאוֹר
Eht Haw Ohr
613 = 200 ר 6 ו 1 א 5 ה   400 ת 1 א
616 Mitzvot

We examine the relationship of The Torah and the number 613. We discover that the 'Light', written of in Genesis 1.1-4 is the Revelation of God as disseminated through 613 Commands. It is not the sun or the moon which were created on day four. We learn that the 613 Commands flow out from the Words God Spoke, 'Let My Light Be Revealed.' We learn of the great importance of the 613 Commands for each of us.

Some Commands are just for B'nei Yisroel / The Children of Israel. Other Commands are for every human on this earth. Some Commands are just for women. Some Commands are just for men. Some Commands are for the Kohan Gadol / the High Priest. Some Commands are just for the Priests. Some Commands are just for the Levites. Some Commands are for just farmers.

Some Commands are just for children. The point is there are 613 Revelations of G-d's Light to us. No one Observes all 613 Commands. Yet each of us are supposed to Observe some of our Creator's Commands.

All that we have flows from the light we have received.

We view the Commands differently based upon our revelation. That is O. K. None of us has the golden key that unlocks the complete intent for each Command from our Creator. G-d Willing we go forward with this understanding.

Eht Ha Orh Everything from the Letter Aleph to the Letter Tav of the the Revelation of Light. I discuss this in more length in Chapter One of my book entitled: <u>Mysterious Signs OF THE TORAH IN GENESIS.</u>

Aleph to Tav - [ת א] When I use the words 'from Aleph to Tav,' I mean 'from the first Letter of the Aleph Bet, the Letter Aleph [א] to the last Letter of the Aleph Bet, the Letter Tav [ת].' The

Eht represents being all inclusive from the beginning of one letter to the conclusion of another letter. *'The word Et is spelled ת א Alef Tav, the first and last letters of the Hebrew alphabet. It therefore implies a transition from beginning to end. Rabbi Ishmael therefore states that its main purpose [in the instance he is referring to] is to indicate the transitive sense of the word "created."*

Rabbi Akiba, on the other hand replies that the very fact that Et contains the Alef Tav implies that it superimposes the entire alphabet between the subject verb and the predicated noun adding all things that pertain to that noun(Cf. Or Torah, Bereisheit). See The Bahir p p 108, 109

Bereisheit Noach

Genesis 6.9 - 11.32

This is the second Parshat of twelve within the book of Genesis. Noach is the Noah of the flood. Noach means *'restful.'*

Bereisheit 6.9

What Is It Like To Be Perfect?

I have heard it said that being perfect is impossible. I have said this and believed this. At one time I believed we were born into a world of sin and that it was impossible to be perfect. That doctrinal line of rubbish teaches followers we can never be good enough for The Lord. No matter what one does they will always have a sinful stench. Well Ha Torah does not Teach this. Ha Torah Teaches the perfection of the individual and the greatness of our soul to draw us close to The Lord God.

Bereisheit 6.9

אֵלֶּה תּוֹלְדֹת נֹחַ נֹחַ אִישׁ צַדִּיק **תָּמִים** הָיָה בְּדֹרֹתָיו אֶת־הָאֱלֹהִים הִתְהַלֶּךְ־נֹחַ׃

Genesis 6.9

These are the generations of Noah; Noah was a just man and ***perfect*** *in his generations, and Noah walked [in every way] from the Letter Aleph to the Letter Tav with God.*

The word תָּמִים Taw Meem means to be whole hearted without blemish. The Bible Says Noach was Perfect in his generation. To me this means Noach was without flaw. There are some that Teach Noach was only perfect because his generation was so evil. In other words Noach was a conditional type of perfection. He wasn't really entirely perfect. I do not believe this. Ha Torah Says Noach was perfect. The Mysticism of perfection is great. The Gematria is 490.

תָּמִים
Taw Meem / Perfect
490 = 40ם 10י 40מ 400ת

I discuss Noach's perfection in my book entitled Dr. Akiva Gamliel Belk, Gematria And Mysticism IN GENESIS Book 2 Chapters 11- 20 (Cedar Hill, Missouri - B'nai Noach Torah Institute, LLC Publishers, 2013)

There is another Gematria that I find most interesting. It is for the Word סלת So Lewht meaning 'Fine Flour'. What could Noach and fine flour have in common? The very first time the Word סלת So Lewht is mentioned in Ha Torah is in Genesis 18.6.

Bereisheit 18.3-8

וַיֹּאמַר אֲדֹנָי אִם־נָא מָצָאתִי חֵן בְּעֵינֶיךָ אַל־נָא
תַעֲבֹר מֵעַל עַבְדֶּךָ׃ יֻקַּח־נָא מְעַט־מַיִם וְרַחֲצוּ
רַגְלֵיכֶם וְהִשָּׁעֲנוּ תַּחַת הָעֵץ׃ וְאֶקְחָה פַת־לֶחֶם
וְסַעֲדוּ לִבְּכֶם אַחַר תַּעֲבֹרוּ כִּי־עַל־כֵּן עֲבַרְתֶּם עַל־
עַבְדְּכֶם וַיֹּאמְרוּ כֵּן תַּעֲשֶׂה כַּאֲשֶׁר דִּבַּרְתָּ׃ וַיְמַהֵר
אַבְרָהָם הָאֹהֱלָה אֶל־שָׂרָה וַיֹּאמֶר מַהֲרִי שְׁלֹשׁ
סְאִים קֶמַח **סֹלֶת** לוּשִׁי וַעֲשִׂי עֻגוֹת׃ וְאֶל־הַבָּקָר רָץ
אַבְרָהָם וַיִּקַּח בֶּן־בָּקָר רַךְ וָטוֹב וַיִּתֵּן אֶל־הַנַּעַר
וַיְמַהֵר לַעֲשׂוֹת אֹתוֹ׃ וַיִּקַּח חֶמְאָה וְחָלָב וּבֶן־הַבָּקָר

אֲשֶׁר עָשָׂה וַיִּתֵּן לִפְנֵיהֶם וְהוּא עֹמֵד עֲלֵיהֶם תַּחַת הָעֵץ וַיֹּאכֵלוּ׃

Genesis 18.3-8

And said, My Lord, if now I have found favor in your sight, pass not away, I beseech you, from your servant; Let a little water, I beseech you, be fetched, and wash your feet, and rest yourselves under the tree; And I will fetch a morsel of bread, and you comfort your hearts; after that you shall pass on; seeing that you are come to your servant. And they said, So do, as you have said. And Abraham hurried to the tent to Sarah, and said, Make ready quickly three measures of fine flour, knead it, and make cakes. And Abraham ran to the herd, and fetched a calf tender and good, and gave it to a young man; and he hurried to prepare it. And he took butter, and milk, and the calf which he had prepared, and set it before them; and he stood by them under the tree, and they ate.

Our Sages Teach the Words לוּשִׁי וַעֲשִׂי עֻגוֹת

meaning Kneed and make cakes actually means to make Matzot. How do we know this?

Shemot 12.39

וַיֹּאפוּ אֶת־הַבָּצֵק אֲשֶׁר הוֹצִיאוּ מִמִּצְרַיִם עֻגֹת מַצּוֹת
כִּי לֹא חָמֵץ כִּי־גֹרְשׁוּ מִמִּצְרַיִם וְלֹא יָכְלוּ
לְהִתְמַהְמֵהַּ וְגַם־צֵדָה לֹא־עָשׂוּ לָהֶם׃

Exodus 12.39

*And they baked **unleavened cakes** of the dough which they brought forth out of Egypt, **for it was not leavened**; because they were thrust out of Egypt, and could not remain, neither had they prepared for themselves any provision.*

We also know that very evening Lot prepared Matzo for his guests. See Genesis 19.3 What is the point? Matzo is bread without leavening. It is the bread of the Holy Temple. It is without sin. Mystically we see that Noach was without sin. We can walk in Noach's steps. We can follow the path of Ha Torah without sinning...

סֹלֶת
Soh Leht
Unleavened Cakes
490 = 400ת 30ל 60ס

Bereisheit Lech Lecha
Genesis 12.1 - 17.27

This is the third Parshat of twelve within the book of Genesis. Lech Lecha means *'Go! Get out!'*

Genesis 13.4

Is Prayer Important?

Who Prays Anymore?

How Did Avram [Abraham] Pray?

Great men like Abram are great for a reason. They have a motive, an incentive, a stimulus, an inspiration. Our Sages Teach us to have proper inducements, i.e. carrots. Abram loved The Lord God! He was a God fearing individual. He faced death and was given life. He faced trials and succeeded. Avram believed and practiced a prayerful life. His descendants followed in his footsteps. Abraham, without making demands or issuing orders or twisting arms, commanded his children and his household after him through prayer.

Bereisheit 13.4

אֶל־מְקוֹם הַמִּזְבֵּחַ אֲשֶׁר־עָשָׂה שָׁם בָּרִאשֹׁנָה וַיִּקְרָא
שָׁם אַבְרָם בְּשֵׁם יְהוָֹה

Genesis 13.4

[Avram went] to the place of the Altar that he built their in the first visit and called their Avram through The Name of The Lord.

Avram is a mystic to us. We follow Avram. We study Avram. A great deal can be learned in doing this. Today we are going to consider how Avram may have called out to The Lord.

The Letter ב Bet in the Word בְּשֵׁם Bih Saym may mean:
in the Name...
with the Name...
through the Name...
There are other possibilities as well.

We are going to consider the possibility of 'through the Name'. When we look at the Word בְּשֵׁם Bih Saym we understand שֵׁם could be in reference to:

The Holy Name...
A designation for The Holy Name...
A place of the Holy Name...
There are other possibilities as well.

We are going to consider the possibility of 'through a designation of the Holy Name'. In this discussion designation would mean Torah.

What is the Gematria of Torah?
תּוֹרָה
Torah
611= 5ה 200ר 6ו 400ת

אַבְרָם בְּשֵׁם יְהוָֹה
Ạvram through The Name of The Lord
243 = 40 = ם 200ר 2ב 1א
342 = 40ם 300ש 2ב
26 = 5ה 6ו 5ה 10י
611 = 26 + 342 +243

Mystically we see Avram crying out to the Creator through Words of Ha Torah. What Words? Perhaps:

Bereisheit 15.1

אַחַר ׀ הַדְּבָרִים הָאֵלֶּה הָיָה דְבַר־יְהוָה אֶל־אַבְרָם בַּמַּחֲזֶה לֵאמֹר אַל־תִּירָא אַבְרָם אָנֹכִי מָגֵן לָךְ שְׂכָרְךָ הַרְבֵּה מְאֹד׃

Genesis 15.1

'...Fear not Avram, I am Your Shield, your reward is very great.'

Bereisheit 12.3

וַאֲבָרְכָה מְבָרֲכֶיךָ וּמְקַלֶּלְךָ אָאֹר וְנִבְרְכוּ בְךָ כֹּל מִשְׁפְּחֹת הָאֲדָמָה׃

Genesis 12.3

I will bless then that bless you...

Notice the Word תִּירָא the Gematria for תִּירָא is 611 also.

תִּירָא

Fear

611 = 1 א 200ר 10י 400ת

[Avram went] to the place of the Altar that he built

there in the first visit and called there Avram through Words of The Torah of The Lord. One could say, [Avram went] to the place of the Altar that he built there in the first visit and called there Avram in fear [awesome respect] of The Lord.

Mystically there are many possibilities. Yet we see the different ways in which one may call out to The Lord.

Bereisheit Vayera

Genesis 18.1 - 22.24

This is the fourth Parshat of twelve within the book of Genesis. Vayera means *'and He Appeared'.*

Bereisheit 18.4, 5

What is A Morsel Of Bread?

The Words of The Lord God are likened to Bread. In Chapter one we began with a discussion of how The Lord God Created the world with Ten utterances. Dear Reader an utterance is like a morsel of bread. An utterance of the Creator is very great and powerful. The Creator Knows the entire meaning of every word in their complete fullness. Every Word Spoken by our Creator includes thought, motion, action, power, creation and much more... So every morsel of bread from The Lord God is entirely and completely loaded from every position / angle. A morsel of bread from The Creator would be unlike any other morsel of bread.

Bereisheit 18.4,5

יֻקַּח־נָא מְעַט־מַיִם **וְרַחֲצוּ רַגְלֵיכֶם** וְהִשָּׁעֲנוּ תַּחַת
הָעֵץ׃

וְאֶקְחָה **פַת־לֶחֶם** וְסַעֲדוּ לִבְּכֶם אַחַר תַּעֲבֹרוּ כִּי־
עַל־כֵּן עֲבַרְתֶּם עַל־עַבְדְּכֶם וַיֹּאמְרוּ כֵּן תַּעֲשֶׂה
כַּאֲשֶׁר דִּבַּרְתָּ׃

Genesis 18.4, 5

Please! Let me take ***a little water and wash your feet*** *while you rest beneath the Tree.*

And I will take take [for you] ***A Morsel of bread*** *to sustain your hearts. Afterwards, continue on. However, this is the reason you passed by your servant. They answered [in unison] Yes! Make like as you said.*

This reason? What is this reason?

The Angels had a reason to stop and to visit with Avraham. The Hebrew Scriptures Say,

Isaiah 52.7
How beautiful upon the mountains are the feet of him who brings good news, who announces peace; who brings good news of good, who announces salvation; who says to Zion, Your God Reigns!

Michael announced Sarah's conception. Raphael brought healing for Avraham. Gabriel salvation for Lot, His wife and children. Rabbi Meir Zlotowitz and Rabbi Nosson Scherman, The Artscroll Tanach Series - Bereishis Vol. I(a) (Brooklyn, New York: Mesorah Publications, Ltd. 3rd Impression, 1989), p 628

Were these the only reasons? Rav Chama bar Chanina said, *It was the third day since Avram's Brit Melah.* It was on the third day our Creator paid a sick call to Avraham. Rabbi Avrohom Davis, The Mesudah Chumash A New Linear Translation Bereishis (Hoboken New Jersey, KTVA Publishing House, Inc., 1991) p 172 Is it possible that on the day of Avraham's brit milah that our Creator dispatched the three angels? Perhaps! Is it possible the three Angels were traveling for three days? Perhaps! I don't know! Yet, we know years later B'nei Yisroel would travel three days without Water, Exodus 15.22. And we know that Water is like Ha Torah. It is from this portion of Ha Torah that we learn we cannot go beyond three days without sharing Ha Torah. Is it possible the Angels stopped to give and receive Words of Ha Torah? Yes! How do we know this?

The Gematria of וְרַחֲצוּ רַגְלֵיכֶם meaning, to take a little water and wash your feet is 613. And we know the Mitzvot / Commands or Observances of Ha Torah are 613.

וְרַחֲצוּ רַגְלֵיכֶם
[to take a little water] and wash your feet
310 = 6ו 90צ 8ח 200ר 6ו
303 = 40ם 20כ 10י 30ל 3ג 200ר
613 = 310 + 303

We also know that the Gematria of פַּת־לֶחֶם meaning A morsel of Bread is the Gematria of 558. What did our Creator Say about Bread?

Deuteronomy 8.3

And he humbled you, and let you hunger, and fed you with manna, which you knew not, neither did your fathers know; that he might make you know that man does not live by bread only, but by every word that proceeds out of the mouth of the Lord does man live.

פַּת־לֶחֶם
Paht Leh Chehm / A morsel of Bread
558 = 40ם 8ח 30ל   400ת 80פ

וּמִצְוֹתָיו
Oov Meezt Vooh Tawv
and [all] His Commandments
558 = 6ו 10י 400ת 6ו 90צ 40מ 6ו

We Observe that the Gematria of וּמִצְוֹתָיו Oov Meezt Vooh Tawv meaning and [all] His Commandments is 558. Mystically this is reference to a morsel of bread. So by this we understand Mystically water is like Torah and the Commandments of our Creator, like a morsel of bread.

Ezekiel 12 Says, '*... Son of man, eat your bread with quaking, and drink your water with trembling and with anxiety....*'

Exodus 1.8 informs us that a new king came into power who did no know Yoseif. In other Words he did not eat the Bread of Mitzvots / Commandments nor drink the Water of Ha Torah... This is what Yoseif did...

Shemot 1.8

וַיָּקָם מֶלֶךְ־חָדָשׁ עַל־מִצְרָיִם אֲשֶׁר לֹא־יָדַע אֶת־יוֹסֵף׃

Exodus 1.8

And there arose up a new king over Egypt, who knew not Joseph.

וַיָּקָם מֶלֶךְ־חָדָשׁ

And there arose up a new king

156 = 40ם 100ק 10י 6ו

402 = 300ש 4ד 8ח   20ך 30ל 40מ

558 = 156 + 402

Bereisheit Chayei Sarah

Genesis 23.1 - 25.18

This is the fifth Parshat of twelve within the book of Genesis. Chayei Sarah means *'the life of Sarah.'*

Bereisheit 23.1 - 25.18

Who is My Soul Mate?

The concept of a Soul Mate is one in which one seeks out and finds the individual that is the perfect fit... the exact fit... in which everything matches. It is as if one soul divided into two. In essence one half of a soul... a being of an individual is seeking the other part of them.

Bereisheit 25.1

וַיֹּסֶף אַבְרָהָם וַיִּקַּח אִשָּׁה וּשְׁמָהּ קְטוּרָה׃

Genesis 25.1

And He, Avraham again ***took his wife*** *and her name was Keturah.*

Our Sages Teach that Avraham took Hagar whose name was changed to Keturah because her deeds were as beautiful / spiritual as קְטֹרֶת incense. Incense rises to the Heavens like one's Spirit. The root for קטר means incense, smoke and to shut one's self in, to enclose. Because of Hagar's attitude she became known as Keturah, the lady with a Spirit like incense or the lady who secluded herself to remain true to her husband. Keturah was was well thought of because she did not seek a divorce from Avraham. And Avraham did not grant Hagar a divorce. The Torah Portion of the Bible Says, וַיְשַׁלְּחֶהָ Vah Yih Shah Lih Cheh Caw, meaning 'And he sent her away.' Hagar was lost without her husband, Avraham. Ha Torah does NOT Say Avraham divorced

Hagar. Sarah did not say to Avraham divorce Hagar. Sarah Said,

Genesis 21.10

[Sarah] Said to Avraham, 'Drive out this slave woman and everything from Aleph to Tav of her son for the son of this slave woman will not inherit with my son with Yitzchok.'

We have NO indication that Avraham divorced Hagar. The marriage bond remained in tack! Our Creator Said to Avraham,

Genesis 21.12

Elohim Said to Avraham, 'Do not consider this wrong in your eyes on account of the boy and your slave woman. Regarding all that Sarah tells you listen to her. For through Yitzchok will seed be considered yours.

The Gematria of וַיִּקַּח אִשָּׁה Vah Yee Kah Ach - Ee Shaw, meaning and he took is 430. The Gematria of נֶפֶשׁ Neh Pehsh / Nefesh meaning

'Soul' is 430. When one takes a wife Mystically we observe he is connecting with a soul. His wife is his Soulmate. How does one know He / she are soul mates? The fact is we are each from the same soul given to us by our Parents of Creation. Still the concept of one's SoulMate being the perfect one... the exact match... the correct fit... is correct. One must understand that perfection is received through marriage. Marriage is an institute where by the husband and wife help to polish the other into what our Creator Intends. The husband and wife work together to form a holy relationship to have a Holy Family with Holy children. The work together to be the single soul God Created them as.

וַיִּקַּח אִשָּׁה
Vah Yee Kah Ach - Ee Shaw, and he took
430 = 5ה 300ש 1א – 8ח 100ק 10י 6ו

נֶפֶשׁ
Neh Pehsh / Nefesh 'Soul'
430 = 300ש 80פ 50נ

Remember: THERE IS A CHOICE! A man or

woman's intent is VERY IMPORTANT. The purpose of taking each other is NOT for just physical sexual pleasure. The Marriage relationship is intended by our Creator to be one of Holiness. Our Creator Blessed the marriage relationship. He did NOT Bless the one night sexual fling!!

Sarah was noted as Avram's Wife. This is an elevated place.

Bereisheit 16.3

וַתִּקַּח שָׂרַי | אֵשֶׁת אַבְרָם אֶת־הָגָר הַמִּצְרִית
שִׁפְחָתָהּ מִקֵּץ עֶשֶׂר שָׁנִים לְשֶׁבֶת אַבְרָם בְּאֶרֶץ
כְּנָעַן וַתִּתֵּן אֹתָהּ לְאַבְרָם אִישָׁהּ לוֹ לְאִשָּׁה:

Genesis 16.3.

Ha Torah Says, 'And Sarai, Avram's wife took...
Why does Ha Torah inform us Sarai was Avram's wife? We already know this. Why not say Sarah took. Why was it necessary to point out Sarah was Avram's wife again? Ha Torah Informs us that Sarai took Hagar to be Avram's wife in

אֵשֶׁת
[Avram's] Wife / His Wife
701 = 400ת 300ש 1א

שְׂאֵת
To Elevate... To Rise...
701 = 400ת 1א 300ש

For a Husband and Wife to reach the lofty Mystical place of being a SoulMate requires elevating the relationship. It requires raising the relationship. Being a 'SoulMate' is not physical. Being a 'SoulMate' is Spiritual!

We continue with several additional points of importance.

What did Avraham do?
וַיַּשְׁכֵּם אַבְרָהָם | בַּבֹּקֶר He got up early in the morning. **Whenever we see Avraham facing a great difficulty we observe these three Words,** וַיַּשְׁכֵּם אַבְרָהָם | בַּבֹּקֶר See Genesis 19.27; 21.14 and 22.3. The first Letter of each Word combined spells שֹׁאֵב Shoh Ayv, meaning to draw as in to draw strength or as in to draw water

(Devarim 29.10) which Mystically means to draw strength from Ha Torah. Sending Yishmael and Hagar away was troubling for Avraham but he did it first thing in the morning. Watching Sedom burn was troubling for Avraham. He arose early in the morning with the hopes there were ten righteous in Sedom. Avraham counted, Lot, Lot's wife, Lot's two married daughters and their husbands, Lot's two daughters who were yet to consummate their marriage and their husbands, a total of 10. When Avraham saw the smoke from the fire it was troubling to him. He felt great anxiety. Avraham arose early to travel to the place where he would offer Yitzchok as an offering. Why? This was deeply troubling to him. וּבְצָרָה Voo Vih Tzraw Rawh, meaning 'And with trouble.' From this we learn that Avraham faced his troubles in the morning. Avraham would draw from the Wells of Torah for Strength. The morning was Avraham's time for prayer. Avraham would seek הָרַחֲמִים Haw Rah Chah Meem, meaning the Mercy [of The Lord]. The Gematria of שֹׁאֵב Shoh Ayv, meaning to draw {from the waters of Ha Torah] is 303. The Gematria of וּבְצָרָה Voo Vih Tzraw Rawh, meaning 'And with trouble.' is 303. The

Gematria of הָרַחֲמִים Haw Rah Chah Meem, meaning the Mercy [of The Lord] is 303.

שֹׁאֵב
Shoh to draw {from the waters of Ha Torah]
303 = 2ב 1א 300ש

וּבְצָרָה
Voo Vih Tzraw Rawh, 'And with trouble.'
303 = 5ה 200ר 90צ 2ב 6ו

הָרַחֲמִים
Haw Rah Chah Meem, the Mercy [of The Lord]
303 = 40ם 10י 40מ 8ח 200ר 5ה

We have discussed how Avraham faced issues that deeply troubled him. Now lets return to considering what a SoulMate is. We have established that The Torah Portion of the Bible does not Say Avraham divorced Hagar. This means they remained married. They remained separated for 38 years. How do we know this? Yitzchok was weaned when Yishmael mocked him, Genesis 21.8 - 14. Our Sages Teach this was after 24 months which is the customary time for a child to suckle, Gittin 75b; Kesuvot 60b. Yitzchok was 40 years of age when he married Rivkah, Genesis 25.20. It was immediately after this Avraham again took his wife Hagar whose name became Keturah.

Bereisheit 25.1

וַיֹּסֶף אַבְרָהָם **וַיִּקַּח אִשָּׁה** וּשְׁמָהּ קְטוּרָה׃

Genesis 25.1

*And He, Avraham again **took his wife** and her name was Keturah.*

I understand אִשְׁתּוֹ is the Word for 'His Wife. Because אִשָּׁה is used the translation would normally would be 'Wife' or 'A Wife'. However Keturah was already Avraham's wife. Therefore this usage means something entirely different than what meets the eye. When Avraham married Hagar she was Sarah's Servant. Notice the Wording carefully!!

Bereisheit 16.2

וַתִּקַּח שָׂרַי ׀ **אֵשֶׁת אַבְרָם** אֶת־הָגָר הַמִּצְרִית
שִׁפְחָתָהּ **מִקֵּץ עֶשֶׂר שָׁנִים לְשֶׁבֶת אַבְרָם בְּאֶרֶץ**

כְּנָעַן וַתִּתֵּן אֹתָהּ לְאַבְרָם אִישָׁהּ לוֹ לְאִשָּׁה:

*Ha Torah Says, 'And Sarai, **Avram's wife** took...* Why does Ha Torah inform us Sarai was Avram's wife? We already know this. Why not say Sarah took. Why was it necessary to point out Sarah was Avram's wife again? Ha Torah Informs us that Sarai took Hagar to be Avram's wife in Genesis 16.3. In Genesis 25.1 Ha Torah Informs us that Avraham took again. Does this mean He took Sarah and now he was taking a wife again? Or does this mean Avram had already taken Hagar and was taking her back again? The Answer has to do with שָׂרַ֫י I אֵשֶׁת אַבְרָם Sarai was the wife of Avram. Hagar was a wife to Avram but not אֵשֶׁת 'his wife' because she belonged to Sarai. This changed when Avram sent Hagar out from his home. Hagar was free. She was no longer Avram's responsibility to care for as a slave. As a result he only gave her bread and water, i.e. Mystically Ha Torah to live on.

Exodus 21.7 - 11

And if a man sells his daughter to be a maidservant, she shall not go out as the menservants do. If she pleases not her master, who has designated her for himself, then shall he let her be redeemed; to sell her to a strange nation he shall have no power, seeing he has dealt deceitfully with her. And if he has betrothed her to his son, he shall deal with her as with a daughter. If he takes for himself another wife; her food, her garment, and her duty of marriage, shall he not diminish. ***And if he does not do these three things to her, then shall she go out free without payment of money.***

Thirty eight years pass. Sarah dies. Yitzchok marries Rivkah. At this point Avraham again takes Hagar. We know it is Hagar because of several Words that are used.

First is וַיֹּסֶף אַבְרָהָם and again Avraham took a wife...

Second is וַיִּקַּח אִשָּׁה 'And he took a wife.' Ha Torah Uses this language to point out this was Hagar, a wife. In Ha Torah 'A Wife' who is owned as a servant is not like a wife that is free. Hagar was NOT אֵשֶׁת אַבְרָם a wife of Avram. Hagar was Sarai's bond maiden. Hagar was a servant wife. She was owned by Sarai. So Sarai gave Hagar to her husband Avram to be a wife not to be אֵשֶׁת אַבְרָם a wife of Avram. So when we see Ha Torah Say וַיֹּסֶף אַבְרָהָם וַיִּקַּח אִשָּׁה *'And He, Avraham again took his wife...'* We understand this is in reference to Hagar, 'a wife' that had already previously been taken. Our Sages point out that Hagar's / Keturah's status is still that of a concubine, i.e. a wife who status is lower than אֵשֶׁת אַבְרָם 'His Wife', Genesis 25.6. Rabbi Avrohom Davis, The Mesudah Chumash A New Linear Translation Bereishis (Hoboken New Jersey, KTVA Publishing House, Inc., 1991) p 267

The Torah portion of the Bible Teaches a man may have more than one wife at the same time. While a Wife may only have one Husband. Why? Does this seem equal? Is this fair? This is not an issue of fairness or equality. It is an issue of mixing seed which is prohibited by the Creator. Now, we are also required to abide by the laws where we reside. Laws that prohibit polygamy must be followed.

One must inquire was Sarah and Keturah each a soulmate with Avraham? Yes! They were Soul Mates from Creation.

Each of us has a Soul Mate / Soul Mates... The disconnect is with the ideology defining a Soul Mate. If one has a rough marriage and the marriage fails does this mean they were not Soul Mates? NO! A soul is that Spiritual being / beings within us. Understand that we each are influenced by the Yetzer Tov / Good Inclination and the Yetzer Raw / Bad Inclination. Our body, mind and soul each are influenced. Life is a journey. If this journey were to take six life cycles one could be married to their Soul Mate in the first lifetime and that marriage may appear like a failure. On the other hand one could be married to their Soul Mate in their sixth life cycle and that marriage would God Willing be greatly enhanced. We don't understand entirely how God Works, how Creation Works or how our body, mind and soul work. However we do know that Ha Torah

Informs us that our soul goes through transmigration. Each transmigration is part of the entire cycle that brings us to a place where each of us are complete and ready to meet our Creator. So when we understand transmigration of the soul we can get a glimpse of how one could have a failed marriage and a divorce yet still be soul mates. Individuals who divorced twenty years ago often see much improvement in their former spouse years later. Yaakov married four sisters. The sisters each shared the same soul. Each sister was a soul mate of Yaakov. The same holds true for brothers. When we read in Genesis 38.8 we see this.

Genesis 38.8
And Judah said to Onan, Go in to your brother's wife, and marry her, and raise up seed to your brother.

Even though we have snapshots of the entire picture about Soul Mates the subject is complicated to us... Remember that the purpose of marriage and the purpose of a soul mate is for all parties to improve, i.e. to be better people.

Bereisheit Toldot

Genesis 25.19 - 28.9

This is the sixth Parshat of twelve within the book of Genesis. Toldot means *'history or generations'*.

Bereisheit 25.19 - 28.9

What Makes A Man the Perfect Husband?

When an individual is greatly motivated to learn and Observe ALL of Ha Torah he / she is following a path of Observances that require excellent behavior. So we look at the evidence. How does one live? We know what The Torah Portion Of The Bible requires so we look for evidence that he / she live by these Observances. We do some research. We check out the individual involved. We watch him or her. Some religions teach that Yaakov was the deceiver yet we know that the real deceiver was his brother Eisov. There are Eisov types who are evil. Ha Torah provides plenty of evidence which reveals who Eisov was when the mask was removed. Then their are individuals who reversed their lives and became Observant. Rahab is an example. Unlike Eisov she did not pretend to Observe Ha Torah. Rahab truly Observed Ha Torah. Ha Tenach says she was a Harlot. Yet through the Observances of Ha Torah her life was reversed and she marries Joshua according to the Jewish Encyclopedia. There are individuals who are real and true and then there are people like Eisov. The Torah Portion of the Hebrew Bible is Speaking about the time when the boys turned age thirteen. Each became a man. Notice the use of the Words אִישׁ Eesh. Eisov is described as a 'cunning man'. Mystically he knew the way of Wisdom. Ha Torah Informs us that Eisov valued Wisdom. With Eisov everything was guarded and calculated based on his accumulated knowledge. Eisov knew how to confuse others. He knew how to trick others. He was skilled in achieving what he wanted by using deceit or through evasive indirect answers. However, Yoh Day Ah can also mean to know one sexually.

Bereisheit 25.27

וַיִּגְדְּלוּ הַנְּעָרִים וַיְהִי עֵשָׂו אִישׁ יֹדֵעַ צַיִד אִישׁ שָׂדֶה וְיַעֲקֹב אִישׁ תָּם יֹשֵׁב אֹהָלִים׃

Genesis 25.27

And the boys grew; and it happened, Esau was ***a man with knowledge,*** *a skilful hunter,* ***a man*** *of the field; and Jacob was a quiet* ***man,*** *living in tents [of Learning].*

We have the Eisov type men. They give the appearance that they are on the path to Ha Torah but what they do shows otherwise. They use Torah Wisdom to <u>only</u> benefit themselves and to take advantage of others.

אִישׁ יֹדֵעַ

eesh Yoh Dah Ah / man with knowledge

395 = 70ע 4ד 10י   300ש 10י 1א

לְהַשְׂכִּיל

Lih Ha Seh Ceel

the path to Wisdom

395 = 30ל 10י 20כ 300ש 5ה 30ל

There is reason The Torah Portion of the Hebrew Bible describes Eisov with the Word Eesh in two different ways. It is like Eisov had two different faces. He has the good inclination and the evil inclination. When we Observe Eisov the man who is described as a farmer we see a man who has gone through a cleansing but still struggles with his impure and evil nature. He says he is going to kill his brother. This is the evil nature. He does not kill his brother. This is the good nature. He is going to meet his brother with 400 servants. His intent seems to be evil yet he hugs his brother and invites him to travel with him. Now we know that even though we see this Gematria shows the clean good side of Eisov we realize he has a very bad side. The Gematria אִישׁ שָׂדֶה Eesh - Saw Deh, meaning, A Man of the Field, A Farmer is 620. The Gematria for being pure is 620.

We have the Eisov type men. They give the appearance that they are clean and pure but what they do shows otherwise. They use Torah as a cover for their actions.

אִישׁ שָׂדֶה
Eesh - Saw Deh
A Man of the Field, A Farmer
620 = 5ה 4ד 300ש 300ש 10י 1א

טְהֹרוֹת
Tih Hoh Roht, Pure Clean
620 = 400ת 6ו 200ר 5ה 9ט

Now lets look at Yaakov. Ha Torah Says Yaakov at the age of manhood, i.e. thirteen was a man without fault. אִישׁ תָּם יֹשֵׁב Now, Tawm means perfect yet we do not translate Yaakov as being Perfect. in comparison Ha Torah Says Noach at the age or 600 was a righteous man perfect in his generation... There are three important points.

Bereisheit 6.9

אֵלֶּה תּוֹלְדֹת נֹחַ נֹחַ אִישׁ צַדִּיק תָּמִים הָיָה בְּדֹרֹתָיו אֶת־
הָאֱלֹהִים הִתְהַלֶּךְ־נֹחַ׃

First

When The Torah portion of the Hebrew Bible Says, נֹחַ אִישׁ צַדִּיק תָּמִים Noach was a righteous man, perfect... this was when Noach was 600 years old. His life of righteousness and perfection were well established over a very long period of time. He was Observed for 600 years. This says a great deal for Noach. In comparison, Yaakov's life was Observed in Ha Torah for only 13 years at the time of this witness.

Second

Noach was married. This means that he was perfect in his marriage. Noach was a father. He was perfect in his relationship to his sons and daughter-in-laws. Yaakov was not married. He did not have any children.

Third

The Word Tawm also means to be finished completely. Is Ha Torah Saying Yaakov was finished... complete? Is Ha Torah Saying Yaakov was Spiritually complete 134 years before he would die? I think Ha Torah is Saying Yaakov had gone as far as a single man could. To go further Yaakov would need a wife. He needed children. He need relatives. How do we know this? The Gematria of תָּם Tawm is 440. The Gematria of תָּמִים Tam Meem is 490. The difference is 50. The

Yud and the Mem are missing from תָּם Tawm. The Gematria for י Yud and ם Mem is 50. Both are at the end of the Word for Perfect. At the time Ha Torah Says Yaakov is תָּם Tawm he was 13 years of age. However, 50 years later when Yaakov was 63 he began seeking a wife, children and relatives. It is like the the Letters Yud and Mem are being added to תָּם Tawm to make him תָּמִים When we Observe Noach we see the Letters Yud and Mem added to תָּם Tawm. They are at the end of the Word. We Observe that Yaakov grew in perfection as he became much older.

Yaakov did not rush into marriage as Eisov did. Yaakov was 77 years of age when he married Leah and Rochel.

Genesis 28.1 - 5

And Isaac called Jacob, and blessed him, and charged him, and said to him, You shall not take a wife of the daughters of Canaan. Arise, go to Padan-Aram, to the house of Bethuel your mother's father; and take a wife from there of the daughters of Laban your mother's brother. And God Almighty bless you, and make you fruitful, and multiply you, that you may be a multitude of people; And give the blessing of Abraham to you, and to your seed with you; that you may inherit the land where you are a stranger, which God gave to Abraham. And Isaac sent away Jacob; and he went to Padan-Aram to Laban, son of Bethuel the Aramean, the brother of Rebekah, Jacob's and Esau's mother.

We learn from Yitzchok's Blessing on Yaakov that he ratified his original Blessing. Yitzchok agreed with his Blessing of Yaakov. Yitzchok's Instructions to Yaakov also indicate his disapproval of his brother Eisov's actions of marrying Canaanite women. He Instructed Yakov to not take a wife from among the Canaanite women. He Instructed Yaakov to take a wife from the daughters of Lavan his mother's brother. He did as his father instructed him.

Soul Mate

Ha Torah is Teaching us who are Jewish that our

Soul Mate will be among B'nei Yisroel or an individual who converts to Torah Observance. Ha Torah is Teaching Noachides to marry another Observant Noachide.

We are going to look at the Mispar Katan of

אִישׁ תָּם Eesh Tawm, A man without fault, this week. God Willing in Parshat Vayishlach we will pick this discussion again.

אִישׁ תָּם

Eesh Tawm, A man without fault

13 = 4ם 4ת 3ש 1י 1א

Another Mispar Katan is קְדָשִׁים Kaw Daw Sheem, Kadoshem, meaning Holiness. Or many holinesses.

קְדָשִׁים

Kaw Daw Sheem / Holiness.

13 = 4ם 1י 3ש 4ד 1ק

A good husband is Holy. This mean he Observes the Mitzvot of Ha Torah. It is the Observance of the Mitzvot that separate him, that dedicate, him that cause him to be moral and of Spiritual

Excellence. He respects the rights of his wife and others in accordance with The Lord God's Commands. This is the real difference between the Eisov's and Yaakov's of the world.

אֲבִי

Ah Vee

Father [like]

13 = 10י 2ב 1א

א – He should love God

ב – He should have a House

י – He should be strong in Observances of Torah

אֲהֵבָה

Ah Hay Vawh

Love - Tenderness... Gentleness... Kindness... Deep Devotion... Sensitivity to pain... Affection... Physical expressions of feeling...

13 = 2ה 2ב 5ה 1א

The Letter ה Hey is found twice in אֲהֵבָה Ah Hay Vawh / Love because the greatest part of being loving is being like the Lord. The comment, 'Love is Divine' is 100% accurate. Be slow to anger. Be gracious. Be long suffering.. be gentle... be faithful... be merciful.

We know that Yaakov loved Rochel so much that he worked fourteen years for her. The first seven years, '*... seemed to him, like a few days because he loved her so much.'*

זֶבֶד

Zeh Vehd, A choice gift... A precious gift... To bestow upon..., to endow with...
13 = 4ד 2ב 7ז

אֶחָד

Echad... to be one
13 = 4ד 8ח 1א

A husband must be one with his wife. He must be extremely sensitive to her needs... to her wants... to her desires... to her conversation... to her soft spoken words... to her tears... to her shouts... to her frustrations...

Yaakov had four wives. He was the husband to the wife he loved, Rochel. He was the husband to the wife he hated, Leah. He was the husband to a concubine wife, Bilhah the half sister of Rochel. He was the husband to a concubine wife, Zilpah the half sister of Leah. He was buried with Leah in the cave of Machpeilah.

Bereisheit Vayeitzei

Genesis 28.10 - 32.3

This is the seventh Parshat of twelve within the book of Genesis. Vayeitzei means *'and he left'*.

Genesis 28.10 - 32.3

What are Actions of Love?

Our Sages Teach that Rochel and Yaakov worked out a code to insure they would not be tricked by Lavan. Yet Rochel could not go through with their plan. Why? Rochel loved her sister Leah. Rochel did not want her older sister to be humiliated in public. It was risky! Yet we do not consider what she did to have harmed her husband. Still, Yaakov at the age of 83 was required to work an additional seven years for a wife that he did not choose and for a wife he did not love... Yaakov was unhappy! Yet he worked these extra seven years because he loved

Rochel. How does their love impact us? David was a descendant of Judah the fourth son of Leah. When one thinks about taking a mate it is good to remember this story. Did Yaakov love Rochel because she was beautiful and sexy or was his love on a much deeper level of Spirituality? Did Yaakov love Rochel because he could see she was loving and kind?

Bereisheit 29.17

וְעֵינֵי לֵאָה רַכּוֹת וְרָחֵל הָיְתָה יְפַת־תֹּאַר וִיפַת מַרְאֶה׃

And Leah was tender eyed, and Rochel was beautifully formed and of beautiful appearance.

Our Sages Teach that Lavan had two daughters and his sister Rivkah had two sons. The older son of Rivkah, Eisov would marry the older daughter of Lavan, Leah and the younger son of Rivkah, Yaakov would marry the younger daughter of Lavan, Rochel. Rabbi Meir Zlotowitz and Rabbi Nosson Scherman, The Artscroll Tanach Series - Bereishis Vol. I(b) (Brooklyn, New York: Mesorah Publications, Ltd. 3rd

Impression, 1989), p 1266

Prayer

Our Sages also Teach that Leah wept when she prayed. Leah would weep and cry out to The Lord that she not be forced to marry the wicked Eisov. Leah's eyes were filled with tears. The tears, prayers and a little deception brought Yaakov to her. Leah loved Yaakov. The Gematria of וְעֵינֵי לֵאָה Vih Ay Nay - Leah, meaning and Leah's Eyes is 182. The Gematria of Yaakov is 182.

וְעֵינֵי לֵאָה

Vih Ay Nay - Leah's Eyes

182 = 5 ה 1 א 30 ל 10 י 50 נ 10 י 70 ע 6 ו

יַעֲקֹב

Yaakov / Jacob

182 = 2 ב 100 ק 70 ע 10 י

Leah altered her course in life through her tearful prayers and her calling out to The Lord... She is the Matriarch.

Rejoicing with One lot in life

The Word רַכּוּת Rah Coht meaning tender or delicate is the Gematria 626. Rah Coht describes Leah's physical condition. Mystically Leah was rejoicing.. exuberant... accelerated... The Gematria for יָשִׂישׂוּ Yaw See Sohv, meaning to rejoice is 626. So even though Leah knew Yaakov loved her sister, Rochel more, she still rejoiced in being married to the righteous Yaakov. Leah loved Yaakov. A sign of love in marriage is rejoicing with one's lot in life..

רַכּוּת

Rah Coht / tender or delicate

626 = 400 ת 6 ו 20 כ 200 ר

יָשִׂישׂוּ

Yaw See Sohv, / to rejoice

626 = 6 ו 300 ש 10 י 300 ש 10 י

Make Every Action A Righteous Action

With Rochel we see a very high quality absolutely necessary in marriage. That quality is defined as 'Doing what is right regardless of how one feels.' This is Spirituality in Marriage. This is Righteousness in marriage. This is a very high level of Love. Yaakov was concerned that Lavan would try to deceive him. Our Sages point to this in Ha Torah when Yaakov Says, 'I will work for you for seven years for Rochel, your younger daughter...' Yaakov was concerned that if he said your daughter Lavan would give him another daughter. Yaakov was concerned that if he said your daughter Rochel that Lavan would change the name of Leah to Rochel so Yaakov said 'Rochel your younger daughter. Still, even after this precaution Yaakov worked out a system of codes which he shared with Rochel so that he would not be deceived. Yet, in the end, Rochel knew of Leah's tears and her prayers and her love for Yaakov. Rochel did not want her sister humiliated in private or public so she gave the special code to Leah. Why did Rochel do this? It is because doing what is right is one of the most important aspects of marriage. This was very risky for Rochel. What if Yaakov became angry with her for sharing this secret code? What if Yaakov chose not to marry her after sharing her secret code? Yet, Rochel humbled herself and honored her older sister. This was both a Spiritual and a Righteous action. On paper Rochel and Yaakov were married. Rochel was Yaakov's wife. Remember the Words Yaakov spoke to Lavan.

Rabbi Moshe Weissman, The Midrash Says (Brooklyn, New York: Benei Yakov Publications 1980), p. 301

Genesis 29. 21

And Yaakov said to Laban, Give me my wife, for my days are fulfilled, that I may consummate my marriage with her.'

Love and Marriage require righteous actions like this. A husband can be wrong. When he is wrong a Righteous Spiritual wife can be of great help. This is an example, and Abigail wife of Nabal is an example, See 1 Samuel 25.

The Gematria of וְרָחֵל Vih Raw Chayl is 244.

The Gematria of צַדִּיקִם Tzah Dee Keem meaning righteous is also 244.

וְרָחֵל

Vih Raw Chayl

244 = 300 ל 8 ח 200 ר 6 ו

References

צַדִּיקִם

Tzah Dee Keem / righteous

244 = 40 ם 100 ק 10 י 4 ד 90 צ

Praise / Worship

Ha Torah Says, וַיֶּאֱהַב יַעֲקֹב אֶת־רָחֵל *'...And He, Yaakov loved everything from the Letter Aleph to the Letter Tav of Rochel.'*

Bereisheit 29. 18

וַיֶּאֱהַב יַעֲקֹב אֶת־רָחֵל וַיֹּאמֶר אֶעֱבָדְךָ
שֶׁבַע שָׁנִים בְּרָחֵל בִּתְּךָ הַקְּטַנָּה׃

And He, Yaakov loved everything from the Letter Aleph to the Letter Tav of Rochel. *And He Said, 'I will work for you for seven years for Rochel, your younger daughter.'*

וַיֶּאֱהַב יַעֲקֹב אֶת־רָחֵל

206 = 2ב 100ק 70ע 10י 2ב 5ה 1א 10י 6ו

639 = 30ל 8ח 200ר 400ת 1א

845 = 206 + 639

תְּהִלָּתִי

Tih Hee law Tee / Praise

845 = 10י 400ת 30ל 5ה 400ת

Yaakov's love for Rochel resulted in her praise for him. Just as great love for one's husband / wife is necessary, so is great praise... One should NEVER speak evil of their mate! The Zohar Speaks of this on a much higher level.

Each of these actions are foundation stones of love in a marriage. The marriage relationship needs mystical ingredients to live and be vibrant.

From Leah we learn prayers with tears can change plans other have made for us. Leah's Love for righteousness is noted in the birth of each child. Relationships established with prayers and tears will have feelings of love and exultation. Those who sow in tears shall reap with joy. Psalms 126.5

From Rochel we learn that The path of the righteous is as a shining light, that shines more and more unto the perfect day, Proverbs 5.18. We learn that love requires both the husband and the wife to do what is right. Love in a relationships depends upon doing what is right.

From Ha Torah we learn that Yaakov greatly loved Rochel. Up until a man marries, his love should focus on his parents. After he marries his love should focus on his wife. Rabbi Meir Zlotowitz and Rabbi Nosson Scherman, <u>The Artscroll Tanach Series - Bereishis Vol. I(a)</u> (Brooklyn, New York: Mesorah Publications, Ltd. 3rd Impression, 1989), p 111

My Wife Makes Me Great

Mystically we Observe that such great love should result in praise. When a man loves his wife properly this will result in her praise. Rabbi Meir Zlotowitz and Rabbi Nosson Scherman, The Artscroll Tanach Series - Bereishis Vol. I(a) (Brooklyn, New York: Mesorah Publications, Ltd. 3rd Impression, 1989), p 104 We learn Psalm 48 surpasses all the other hymns of praise for our Creator. This Psalm was sung in praise of our Creator, our King, by the Community of Israel. Yet, if the Psalm is not sung where is the praise? In the words, "The Lord is Great and highly exalted... We learn this is true when His People praise Him. We learn a King without praise is no king. Thus, a husband is nothing without his wife's praise. Yaakov had four wives... yet without their praise he was as nothing! Our Sages Teach he is not included in the category of "man", nor is he even worthy to be blessed. Rab Hamnuna the Elder, stated Job was called 'great' only because of his wife, who was God-fearing like himself... Job 1.3. Zohar C 5a

Bereisheit Vayishlach

Genesis 32.4 - - 36.43

This is the eight Parshat of twelve within Genesis. Vayishlach means *'and he sent'.*

Bereisheit 32.4,5

Who Are The People of the Covenant?

We read of Leah and Rochel but what about Bilhah and Zilpah? Are they also people of the Covenant. If we are to use today's measuring stick we would have to say yes! After all who would consider Dan or Naftali were Jewish if only their father Yaakov was Jewish. What about Gad or Asher were they Jewish. Based upon today's standards it is possible that Dan, Naftali Gad or Asher would be accepted as being Jewish if only one parent was Jewish. We don't read in Ha Torah of Leah, Rochel Bilhah or Zilpah having gone through a convert's course. We call Lavan an evil person yet he was the other grandfather. During the formative years all of Yaakov's children were raised around Lavan and his wicked sons. Rochel dies early in life. Yaakov loses all his wives before journeying to Mitzriam at 130 years of age. Yet his children turn out well for the most part. They come from very unique beginnings yet each son becomes the head of one of the twelve tribes. This is really quite remarkable. These sons are the forefathers of B'nei Yisroel. So even though we, the Jewish people are the chosen we come from a group of nomads who, despite their uniqueness, loved and honored The Lord God and as a result became the people God selected to receive Ha Torah. We are really blessed to be counted among them.

Bereisheit 32.4,5

וַיִּשְׁלַח יַעֲקֹב מַלְאָכִים לְפָנָיו אֶל־עֵשָׂו אָחִיו אַרְצָה
שֵׂעִיר שְׂדֵה אֱדוֹם׃ וַיְצַו אֹתָם לֵאמֹר כֹּה תֹאמְרוּן
לַאדֹנִי לְעֵשָׂו כֹּה אָמַר עַבְדְּךָ יַעֲקֹב עִם־לָבָן **גַּרְתִּי**
וָאֵחַר עַד־עָתָּה׃

Genesis 32.4.5

*And Jacob sent Messengers / Angels before him to Eisov, his brother to the land of Seir, the country of Edom. And he commanded them, saying, Thus shall you speak to my lord Eisov; Your servant Yaakov said thus, **I have been a stranger** with Laban, and stayed there until now, [as a stranger to his ways.]*

גַּרְתִּי

Gar Tee / I have been a Stranger

613 = 10ט 400ת 200ר 3ג

The Observances of Ha Torah are 613.

Did Yaakov keep the 613 Observances? Some of our Sages Teach that this Mystical statement he made to Eisov is to be interpreted as he kept all the Observances.

When One Observes the 613 Mitzvot they are strange. One does not try to be strange. One is strange.

Modesty - How we dress is strange. Our style is a shirt with sleeves and long slacks for men and a blouse with sleeves and a long skirt for women. Some ladies wear pants especially designed for women. The purpose is to cover the body. Men wear a Kippah to acknowledge God as Creator of the universe. Women wear a head covering to conceal their crown, i.e. their natural hair from everyone but their husband so they can be a glory only to him.

Our conversation is Tiferet / Beautiful. We are not supposed to speak evil of others. We are supposed to not cause pain with words. We are not supposed to gossip.

Isaiah 52.1
Awake, awake; put on your strength, O Zion; put on your beautiful garments...

Exodus 22.20
You shall not wrong a stranger, nor oppress him; for you were strangers in the land of Egypt.

Oppressing a stranger is called אוֹנָאַת דְּבָרִים Oh Naw Aht - Dih Vaw Reem, meaning to cause pain with words...

Vayikra 19.16

לֹא־תֵלֵךְ רָכִיל בְּעַמֶּיךָ לֹא תַעֲמֹד
עַל־דַּם רֵעֶךָ אֲנִי יְהוָה :

Leviticus 19.16
Do not go about as a talebearer...

Leviticus 19.2
Speak to all the congregation of the people of Israel, and say to them, You shall be holy; for I the Lord your God am holy.

In other words we are not to be participants of wrong actions around us. We are to live Holy lives. We are to be separated from the rest of our world. How do we do this? We Observe the 613 Commands that pertain to us...

Bereisheit 33.20

וַיַּצֶּב־שָׁם מִזְבֵּחַ וַיִּקְרָא־לוֹ
אֵל אֱלֹהֵי יִשְׂרָאֵל :

Genesis 33.20

And he erected there an altar, and called Oh Almighty God of Yisroel.

אֵל אֱלֹהֵי יִשְׂרָאֵל

Almighty God of Yisroel

77 = 10י 5ה 30ל 1א   30ל 1א

541 = 30ל 1א 200ר 300ש 10י

618 = 77 + 541

בהתורה

Bih Ha Torah / In The Torah

618 = 5 ה 200ר 6ו 400ת 5ה 2ב

Who are the People of the Covenant?

Bereisheit 32.29

וַיֹּאמֶר לֹא יַעֲקֹב יֵאָמֵר עוֹד שִׁמְךָ
כִּי אִם־יִשְׂרָאֵל כִּי־שָׂרִיתָ עִם־אֱלֹהִים
וְעִם־אֲנָשִׁים וַתּוּכָל׃

Genesis 33.29

And He [the angel / the messenger related what God] Said, 'Your name shall be called no more Jacob, because [you are to be the] nation Israel; for as a prince you have power with God and with men, and have prevailed.'

This was the foretelling of the coming birth of Benjamin, i.e. the twelfth son.

כִּי אִם־יִשְׂרָאֵל
because [you are to be the] nation Israel
71 = 40ם 1א   10י 20כ
541 = 30ל 1א 200ר 300ש 10י
612 = 71 + 541

We Observe this again just before the birth of Benjamin.

Bereisheit 35.10

וַיֹּאמֶר־לוֹ אֱלֹהִים שִׁמְךָ יַעֲקֹב לֹא־יִקָּרֵא
שִׁמְךָ עוֹד יַעֲקֹב כִּי אִם־יִשְׂרָאֵל
יִהְיֶה שְׁמֶךָ וַיִּקְרָא אֶת־שְׁמוֹ יִשְׂרָאֵל׃

Genesis 35.10

And God Said to him, 'Your name is Jacob; your name shall not be called Jacob any more, because [you are to be the] nation Israel, and it was his name. And He Called Everything from the Letter Aleph to the Letter Tav of his name Yisroel.

בְּרִית
Bih Reet / Covenant
612 = 400ת 10י 200ר 2ב

175 - Abraham
180 - Yitzchok
147 - Yaakov
110 - Yoseif
612

Exodus 34.23
שָׁלֹשׁ פְּעָמִים בַּשָּׁנָה יֵרָאֶה כָּל־זְכוּרְךָ אֶת־פְּנֵי הָאָדֹן
יְהוָה אֱלֹהֵי יִשְׂרָאֵל׃

Exodus 34.23
Three times in the year shall all your males appear before the Lord God, the God of Israel.

יְהוָה אֱלֹהֵי יִשְׂרָאֵל
Lord God Of Yisroel
72 = 10י 5ה 30ל 1א   5ה 6ו 5ה 10י
541 = 300ל 1א 200ר 300ש 10י
613 = 72 + 541

So Dear Ones, we Observe through the Mysticism of the Gematria of 613 that our Creator is the God of Yisroel. We Observe the Gematria of the Covenant and the lives of Avraham, Yitzchok, Yaakov and Yoseif equal 612. Mystically we Observe that God Chose Yisroel to be a nation of people that would serve Him. We Observe through the Gematria of 618 He is the Almighty God of Yisroel. This is the same Gematria of 'Being in the Torah".

Bereisheit Vayeishev

Genesis 37.1 - 40.22

This is the ninth Parshat of twelve within the book of Genesis. Vayeishev means *'and he settled'.*

Bereisheit 37.3

What is the Price of Love, Hate, Jealousy and For the Righteous?

Yoseif was a righteous man. He was a messenger of God. He received prophecy from The Creator. What do you think it would have been like to have been a brother of Yoseif? What would it be like to have a prophetic father like Yaakov and Yitzchok and Avraham when the world was a much smaller place when the population was less than a few million? What would it be like for a member of our family to be the Messenger of God? However, Dear Ones, in the eye of eternity our ancestors were not all that distant. Yet we view them as long gone. Reading about them is odd because Genesis is not a story book but a book of the history of who we descended from. How do we construct that bridge from today back a few thousand years to Yoseif?

For me, when my eyes are opened to a Gematria which is new to me, I am excited. It is a special feeling... a special minute... I have studied through Bereisheit dozens of times yet there is always something around the corner waiting to be rediscovered. I am honored to share the Gematria's the Creator reveals, May His Name Be Blessed and Praised! This makes one feel special. Yoseif felt special. Yaakov made this special colorful tunic for him. Wow! Yoseif was given dreams and visions and prophecy. Even though we may not receive dreams, or visions, or prophecy, or Gematria everything one receives from the Creator is special. I am thankful for those 18 hour... 24 hour... periods of studies and more and for the nights I was awakened to learn Gematria. This has enriched by life... and I am deeply thankful. Blessed is His Name!!

Bereisheit 37.3

וְיִשְׂרָאֵל אָהַב אֶת־יוֹסֵף מִכָּל־בָּנָיו כִּי־בֶן־זְקֻנִים
הוּא לוֹ וְעָשָׂה לוֹ כְּתֹנֶת פַּסִּים׃

Genesis 37.3

And Yisroel loved everything from the first Letter Aleph to the last Letter Tav of Yoseif more than all his sons because he was a son of old age ***to him.*** *[Yisroel] made a tunic of fine wool* ***to him.***

This action of their father, Yisroel making the Tunic for Yoseif confirmed to all the sons that he loved Yoseif more than all of them. They were envious and jealous! We see the emphasis of the Word לו Loh, meaning 'to him' being repeated twice. The Gematria of Loh is 36. The Gematria of Leah is also 36. There is a direct path here of what it feels like to be loved or hated. Ha Torah Says, *'...[Yisroel] loved Rochel more than Leah...'*, Genesis 29.28. *The Lord Saw that Leah was the hated one and he opened her womb. Rochel remained barren,* Genesis 29.31. After Yisroel's first son Reuvein was born

Ha Torah quotes Leah as having said, *'... The Lord Has Seen my affliction: for now my husband will love me',* Genesis 29.32. When Leah's second son was born to Yisroel she said, *'Since The Lord Heard that I am the hated one He also Gave this one,'* Genesis 29.33 .Ha Torah records Leah's comments after having a third son, *'[Maybe] this time my husband will become attached to me,'* Genesis 29.34. After her sixth son she said, '...now [Maybe] my husband will make his [main] home with me...', Genesis 30.21. There are several points we take from this.

1.) 'He loved Rochel more than Leah' - This was obvious.

2.) 'The Lord Saw Leah was the hated one... the despised one... the disliked one... the abhorred one...' Leah could feel, and The Lord could see an intense dislike... a passionate dislike... given off by Yaakov.

3.) '...now my husband will love me... Leah did not feel love coming from Yaakov. She did not feel deep affection from Yaakov. There was no romance.

4.) 'The Lord Has Heard that I am the hated one...' Yaakov was a righteous man yet even though he tried very much to hide his dislikes for Leah they were obvious. He tried to treat her well yet Tents are made out of cloth. Words of passion travel. Noise travels. The passion and excitement he felt for Rochel was noticeably lacking with Leah. He kept his main home with Rochel. Then after her death he kept his main home with Bilhah. This was an insult to Reuvein. He moved his father's bed. Rabbi Avrohom Davis, The Mesudah Chumash A New Linear Translation Bereishis (Hoboken New Jersey, KTVA Publishing House, Inc., 1991) p 401 The Gematria connection of 36 points to the love Yaakov felt for Rochel and Yoseif and the hate Yaakov felt for Leah. Even though Rochel was now gone, Yisroel felt great love for her, and that love that Leah greatly desired was now showered on Yoseif.

לוֹ
Loh, / 'to him'
36 = 6ו 30ל

לֵאָה
Leah
36 = 5ה 1א 30ל

The Torah Says, 'Rochel was Jealous of her sister... [Leah for having sons]' Genesis 30.1 and that Yoseif's brothers were jealous of him, Genesis 37.11.

So we have this dimension of love, hate and jealousy within Yaakov's righteous family.

Bereisheit 37.4

וַיִּרְאוּ אֶחָיו כִּי־אֹתוֹ אָהַב אֲבִיהֶם
מִכָּל־אֶחָיו **וַיִּשְׂנְאוּ אֹתוֹ** וְלֹא
יָכְלוּ דַּבְּרוֹ לְשָׁלֹם׃

Genesis 37.4

And [Yoseif's] brothers saw that their father loved him more than all his brothers ***and they hated him*** *and they could not speak peaceable to him.*

The Gematria 36 and 780 reveals Mystical answers from within Ha Torah about Love, Hatred and Jealousy.

וַיִּשְׂנְאוּ אֹתוֹ
Vah Yees Nih Voo Oh Tov / And they hated
373 = 6ו 1א 50נ 300ש –1י 6ו
407= 6ו 400ת 1א

780 = 373 + 407

Who was this hatred directed towards? Yoseif. Yoseif? Why was Yoseif hated? In part because of the interpretations of his dreams. The Gematria of פִּתְרֹנִים Pee Tih Roh Neem meaning interpretations is thew Gematria of 780.

פִּתְרֹנִים
Pee Tih Roh Neem / interpretations
780 = 40ם 10י 50נ 200ר 400ת 80פ

So even though Yoseif's interpretations were true he was hated.
Ha Torah Informs us that Yoseif's brothers were jealous... envious of him.. resentful towards him...

begrudging of him... they were covetous of what Yoseif had. The Creator of the Universe Gave Yoseif dreams. The brothers were keenly aware of their father Yaakov's dreams. Remember, Ha Torah records one of Yaakov's famous dreams. Yaakov dreamed of a ladder extended between heaven and earth with Angels ascending and descending. The brothers did not receive dreams. They understood this as a sign. Yaakov received dreams. Yoseif received dreams. They did not receive dreams. They had the ability to interpret dreams as did their father and Yoseif. However Yoseif appeared to be on a higher Spiritual plain. Then Yoseif was loved by their father. Yisroel's love for Yoseif was strong. He made a tunic for him. Yoseif was the envoy between his father and brothers.

Ha Torah informs that the brothers were jealous of Yoseif's dreams.

Bereisheit 37.11

וַיְקַנְאוּ־בוֹ אֶחָיו וְאָבִיו שָׁמַר אֶת־הַדָּבָר׃

Genesis 37.11

And his brothers [were jealous] envied him;
but his father kept the matter in mind.

The Gematria of וַיְקַנְאוּ־בוֹ אֶחָיו is 206.

וַיְקַנְאוּ־בוֹ אֶחָיו
Vah Yih Kay Nih Voo Voh Eh Chawv
And His brother were Jealous
173 = 1ו 1א 50נ 100ק 10י 6ו
33 = 6ו 10י 8ח 1א 6ו 2ב
206 = 173 + 33

רֹאֶה
Roh Eh / To See
206 = 5ה 1א 200ר

דִּבֶּר
Dee Bawr / To sSpeak
206 = 200ר 2ב 4ד

Genesis 37.18-20
And when they saw him from far away, even before he came near to them, they conspired against him to slay him. And they said one to another, Behold, this dreamer comes.

Come now therefore, and let us slay him, and throw him into some pit, and we will say, Some evil beast has devoured him; and we shall see what will become of his dreams.

The brothers became very jealous because they could see their father's love for Yoseif was much greater than his love for them. They could see the Creator Gave Yoseif dreams as He Gave their father dreams. Yoseif spoke evil about his brothers in his reports to their father. Yoseif spoke of his dreams. These actions brought on Jealousy. The brothers were so upset they spoke of murdering Yoseif. This was a very powerful jealousy. They were angry with their father. The dipping of Yoseif's tunic in blood was directed at their father's love for Yoseif. They were rebelling against Yaakov's greater love for Yoseif and lesser love for them. They were rebelling against Yaakov's greater love for Rochel and lesser love for Leah, Bilhah and Zilpah. The brothers were angry at their father.

The strangest part is, we do not see any

indication that they were jealous of their father's learning Ha Torah with Yoseif and Benjamin. They were jealous of the colorful Tunic, i.e. under garment. They were jealous of Yoseif's colorful Tallit Katan. It was like an undershirt. It was hidden. They would notice it when Yoseif used the mikvah. He would have to remove his clothing to immerse in the water. This hidden prayer shawl was a sign to them that Yaakov loved Yoseif more than them. He favored Yoseif.

Genesis 37.31
They took Yoseif's tunic, slaughtered a goat and dipped the tunic in the blood. [Then] they sent the long colorful tunic and brought it to their father, and said , 'We found this. Please identify it. Is it your son's tunic or not?'

They were not supposed to know about the tunic. I think this tunic was like Yaakov's tunic and that is what upset the brothers. Just the same they were being very disrespectful to Yaakov, their father. The brothers thought that stripping Yoseif of his inner prayer tunic and selling him into slavery, i.e. splitting him and his father up would stop Yoseif's scary prayerful visions. This did not stop his prayerful visions. This shows that THE BROTHERS WERE ALSO ANGRY WITH GOD!!

Genesis 37.5-11

And Joseph dreamed a dream, and he told it to his brothers; and they hated him even more. And he said to them, I request you to hear this dream which I have dreamed; For, behold, we were binding sheaves in the field, and, lo, my sheaf arose, and also stood upright; and, behold, your sheaves stood around, and made obeisance to my sheaf. And his brothers said to him, Shall you indeed reign over us? or shall you indeed have dominion over us? And they hated him even more for his dreams, and for his words. And he dreamed yet another dream, and told it his brothers, and said, Behold, I have again dreamed a dream; and, behold, the sun and the moon and the one and ten stars made obeisance to me. And he told it to his father, and to his brothers; and his father rebuked him, and said to him, What is this dream that you have dreamed? Shall I and your mother and your brothers indeed come to bow down ourselves to you to the earth? And his brothers envied him; but his father kept the matter in mind.

Dear Ones, eleven is not the proper interpretation even though ten plus one equals eleven. When translators just jump to eleven, the important meaning is excluded. When Ha Torah Says one, this is in reference to Benjamin who was not part of the rebellion against God or Yaakov. The ten is in reference to the ten brothers who did rebel against God because they were angry. So One and ten have very important meaning which is lost by translating this as eleven.

Bereisheit 37.9

וַיַּחֲלֹם עוֹד חֲלוֹם אַחֵר וַיְסַפֵּר אֹתוֹ לְאֶחָיו וַיֹּאמֶר
הִנֵּה חָלַמְתִּי חֲלוֹם עוֹד וְהִנֵּה הַשֶּׁמֶשׁ וְהַיָּרֵחַ **וְאַחַד**
עָשָׂר כּוֹכָבִים מִשְׁתַּחֲוִים לִי׃

Bereisheit 37.20

וְעַתָּה ׀ לְכוּ וְנַהַרְגֵהוּ וְנַשְׁלִכֵהוּ בְּאַחַד הַבֹּרוֹת

וְאָמַרְנוּ חַיָּה רָעָה אֲכָלָתְהוּ וְנִרְאֶה
מַה־יִּהְיוּ חֲלֹמֹתָיו:

תְּפִלִּין
Tih Fee Leen / Prayer, i.e. the Phylacteries worn by men during prayer...
570 = 50ן 10י 30ל 80פ 400ת

עָשָׂר
Aw Sawr / The Ten [rebellious sons who wanted to stop Yoseif's prayerful dreams / visions] Benjamin is not included. This is the difference between the interpretation of one and ten instead of eleven...
570= 200ר 300ש 70ע

מַה־יִּהְיוּ חֲלֹמֹתָיו
Mah - Yee Hih Voo - Chah Loh Moh Tawv
What will happen to Yoseif's dreams [after he is dead or sold into slavery]?
76 = 6ו 10י 5ה 10י 5ה 40מ
494 = 6ו 10י 400ת 40מ 30ל 8ח
570 = 76 + 494

Because of their anger, jealousy and hate the ten brothers tried to silence Yoseif's prayerful dreams and visions. But they were not silenced!! They were angry with the Lord God's Messenger! Still God brought the dreams to pass.

Bereisheit 50.19,20

וַיֹּאמֶר אֲלֵהֶם יוֹסֵף אַל־תִּירָאוּ כִּי
הֲתַחַת אֱלֹהִים אָנִי׃
וְאַתֶּם חֲשַׁבְתֶּם עָלַי **רָעָה** אֱלֹהִים חֲשָׁבָהּ לְטֹבָה
לְמַעַן עֲשֹׂה כַּיּוֹם הַזֶּה לְהַחֲיֹת עַם־רָב׃

Genesis 50.19,20

And Joseph said to them, Fear not; for am I in the place of God?

But as for you, you thought ***evil against me****; but God* ***meant it for good****, to bring to pass, as it is this day, to save much people alive.*

We observe the 570 in their actions were meant for evil but God changed their evil actions to good. And all was well! God reversed the outcome. God made it turn out good.

Mikeitz

Genesis 41.1 - 44.17

This is the tenth Parshat of twelve within the book of Genesis. Mikeitz means *'at the end.'*

Bereisheit 41.1

Why is a Dream Like Bread and Salt?

Bread, i.e. The Word of God feeds us. Salt preserves us. Dreams do the same thing. Look at Pharaoh's dream. It was powerful. He understood his dream had great significance. He was troubled by what he did not know. He was self assured. He was not threatened by bringing a prisoner out of jail and making him Viceroy of his vast empire. His dream was so troubling he had to have the answer. How is it possible that a prisoner would hold the interpretation... the answer to what troubled him? How is it that the very best interpretations money could afford could not give Pharaoh an answer which would satisfy his soul? They did not have the right words. Their words were not the Words of The Lord. Their words did not feed or preserve. It's like a lock and key to a degree. Many keys may fit into the lock but only the right key opens the lock. The Lord God made Yoseif that key for Pharaoh. In the same way if we are willing to be fashioned, our Creator can shape us into the key that helps others by bringing bread, i.e. The Word of The Lord into their lives. We can be the key that helps preserve the lives of others.

Bereisheit 41.1

וַיְהִ֕י מִקֵּ֖ץ שְׁנָתַ֣יִם יָמִ֑ים וּפַרְעֹ֣ה חֹלֵ֔ם
וְהִנֵּ֖ה עֹמֵ֥ד עַל־הַיְאֹֽר׃

Genesis 41.1

And it happened after two years of days and ***Pharaoh had a dream*** *and behold he was standing on the bank of the river.*

Ha Torah Says Pharaoh had a dream. In actuality The Lord God Communicated with Pharaoh. When The Lord God Communicates with us this is called חֹלֵם Choo Laym, i.e. a dream, a vision. Sometimes we receive other types of communications. These communications are not from The Lord God. These communications are NOT dreams. They are nightmares. When my students have a dream or a nightmare I Teach my students to say 'I have had a dream or I have had a nightmare' to another student or relative or friend who has been schooled properly in the response to dreams and nightmares. After hearing this confession of a dream or nightmare the individual who is properly schooled in responding to a dream or nightmare IMMEDIATLY SAYS, May only good dreams come to pass. What did Yoseif Say to Pharaoh? 'God Will Respond to Pharaoh in peace.

Yoseif was an interpreter. Few are interpreters. We who are not interpreters simply say, 'May only good dreams come to pass.' We don't guess at the interpretation. I have dreamed dreams that no one could interpret. One particular dream was not meant to be interpreted then. The interpretation was intended to be given twenty years later.

Numbers 12.6
And He [The Lord God] Said, 'Hear now My Words; If there is a prophet among you, I the Lord Will Make Myself known to him in a Vision, and Will Speak to him in a Dream.

Receiving a Vision, a Dream or interpreting A Vision or a Dream is a very special communication from our Creator. A Dream is Mystical and Spiritual. Why? The Final Letter Mem is mystical... The Letter Chof is Spiritual...

חֹלֵם
Choo Laym, / a Dream a Vision.
78 = 40ם 30ל 8ח

לֶחֶם
Leh Chem / Bread
78 = 40ם 8ח 30ל

מֶלַח
Meh Lah Ach / Salt
79 = 8ח 30ל 40מ

Bread sustains, salt preserves, dreams

communicate. It all depends on how the Holy Letters are arranged.

Years ago, before returning to Torah Observance, back in 5740 (1980) I was appointed by my Daddy to manage the family property. This meant the cleaning, painting, repairing and renting, etc., was all my responsibility. My family owned a beautiful two bedroom bungalow several blocks away from Washington Park, now known as the 'Wash Park Area'. My younger brothers grew up in this older home. My family purchased another property to live in back in the hills of Missouri. It was my responsibility to make our former home ready to lease. It needed to be prepped for painting on the inside. There was enough money in the budget to hire a professional painter. Instead I chose to take on the job myself. After all, my Daddy and my Mommy, may they rest in peace, my brothers and I had painted many apartments and houses over the years. This was something I was acquainted with. It did not seem that difficult. However I made it difficult... extremely difficult!!

I got impatient. I was in a hurry to get started. I wanted to knock the job out in one day. Those hired to cover the mantle, windows, hardwood floors and other areas were moving much too slow for this impatient kid. I wish I had the energy from back then...They were doing a very good job but I was impatient. After awhile I could take no more. I hooked up the high pressure sprayer and began spraying everything in sight. Unfortunately this included many areas that should not have been sprayed. The pressure was not correct. The paint mixture was wrong. Many areas had considerable over spray like the oak hardwood floors, window panes, mirrors, ceramic tile, sinks, door handles, etc. I made a real mess of things! This was very embarrassing! My only solace was that all of my family was out of town for awhile.

I began trying to clean up the over spray. It only got worse. I wanted to bury my face in my hands and cry. Later that evening, after hours of work, I gave up and went home realizing this was not going to go away without a miracle. Have you every wanted to take back a deed? Have you ever wanted to relive a day? Well...

Late that night I cried, *'Oh Lord please help me. Look at what I have done. My Daddy is going to kill me. What a sad thing to do! I need your help! What am I going to do'?*

That night I had a dream... I had a vision of a television commercial. It was a short dream. All I saw was the name... the label on a white plastic cleaning bottle. Then I heard these words, *'Remember what happened when you used that product [to clean the dirt from around the light switches]'?* I remembered spraying the wall around the dirty area. The spray rolled down the wall removing the dirt and some of the paint also. Obviously the product name is omitted for a reason.

The next morning I instructed my helpers to purchase that product and hurry over to the house. We sprayed it on the hardwood floors then let it settle several minutes. The paint wiped clean! I shouted *Thank G-d!'* We used this spray to clean the paint off of everything. The nightmare was finally under control. The Creator came to my rescue through a dream.

Holy Reader, The Lord Uses visions to give us clarity. It is like The Lord Says,*'Quiet on the set! Action! Roll 'em!'* Then the picture begins to play. It was like The Lord gave me a self-help... instructional video... Dear Ones, in a more profound way The Lord Showed Moshe every detail on how to create the Menorah from Aleph to Tav that we read about in this Parshat.

Genesis 20.1-18
And Abraham journeyed from there toward the Negev, and lived between Kadesh and Shur, and sojourned in Gerar. And Abraham said of Sarah his wife, She is my sister; and Abimelech king of Gerar sent, and took Sarah. But God came to Abimelech ***in a dream*** *by night, and said to him, Behold, you are but a dead man, because of the woman whom you have taken; for she is a man's wife. But Abimelech had not come near her; and he said, Lord, will you slay also a righteous nation? Said he not to me, She is my sister? and she, even she herself said, He is my brother; in the integrity of my*

heart and innocency of my hands have I done this. And God said to him ***in a dream,*** *Yes, I know that you did this in the integrity of your heart; for I also kept you from sinning against me; therefore I did not let you touch her. Now therefore restore the man his wife; for he is a prophet, and he shall pray for you, and you shall live; and if you restore her not, know you that you shall surely die, you, and all who are yours. Therefore Abimelech rose early in the morning, and called all his servants, and told all these things in their ears; and the men were very afraid. Then Abimelech called Abraham, and said to him, What have you done to us? And in what have I offended you, that you have brought on me and on my kingdom a great sin? You have done deeds to me that ought not to be done. And Abimelech said to Abraham, What did you see, that you have done this thing? And Abraham said, Because I thought, Surely the fear of God is not in this place; and they will slay me for my wife's sake. And yet indeed she is my sister; she is the daughter of my father, but not the daughter of my mother; and she became my wife. And it came to pass, when God caused me to wander from my father's house, that I said* *to her, This is your kindness which you shall show to me; at every place where we shall come, say of me, He is my brother. And Abimelech took sheep, and oxen, and menservants, and women servants, and gave them to Abraham, and returned to him Sarah his wife. And Abimelech said, Behold, my land is before you; live where it pleases you. And to Sarah he said, Behold, I have given your brother a thousand pieces of silver; behold, he is to you a covering of the eyes, to all who are with you, and with all other; thus she was reproved. And Abraham prayed to God; and God healed Abimelech, and his wife, and his maidservants; and they bore children. For the Lord had fast closed up all the wombs of the house of Abimelech, because of Sarah Abraham's wife.*

In the above verses are the first and second times in the Torah Portion of The Hebrew Bible where the Word בַּחֲלוֹם Bah Chah Lom, meaning, in a dream occurs. The Gematria of בַּחֲלוֹם is 86. The Gematria for the Word אֱלֹהִים Elohim, God is the Gematria 86. Notice the special relationship between the one who dreams and God our Creator the Giver of Dreams

בַּחֲלוֹם
Bah Chah Lom / In A Dream
86 = 40ם 6ו 30ל 8ח 2ב

אֱלֹהִים
Elohim / God
86 = 40ם 10י 5ה 30ל 1א

The next time that you receive a Dream stop and consider it. Why did I have this dream. Is this Dream a Vision from our Creator? Is this dream a nightmare, a hallucination? Explore the Dream. Think on it. Don't pass it by. Ask, What is the message? What is the purpose. Dear Ones, it is important be sensitive to Dreams. Dreams are often a communication from God. Dreams carry important messages.

Receiving a Dream from God is an awesome experience.

ב ה

Vayigash

Genesis 44.18 - 47.27

This is the eleventh Parshat of twelve within the book of Genesis. Vayigash means *'and he approached.'*

Bereisheit 47.27

How Did Yisroel Dwell In Mitzrim?

This discussion is about learning to be Blessed while dwelling in a situation and in a place you do not want to be in. Even though your situations are different this describes many of us.

Life has places where the shoes are a bit tight. It may be to much of a stretch for us to imagine what it was like for an older man, a widower, a man who mourned the loss of his son 22 years to travel by wagon from Eretz Canaan to Mitzraim at the age of 130. Yet this is what Yaakov did. He left his home in Eretz Canaan. Does anyone understand how difficult it was for Yaakov to leave his home, the home he finally settled in after decades of being displaced. He would have spent his last days their in the land of his father and Grandfather but famine disrupted his plans. Yoseif his first born of Rochel disrupted his plans. Yaakov had great wealth. He had many cattle. Even with the famine he may have been able to comfortably live out his days without traveling to Mitzraim. Yet Yaakov did what most seniors do not want to think of doing, i.e. moving away from the home they love in old age and to go live with a son. How did this feel to him? We do not read of objections. Yaakov seemed content to do this.

Bereisheit 47.27

וַיֵּשֶׁב יִשְׂרָאֵל בְּאֶרֶץ מִצְרַיִם בְּאֶרֶץ גֹּשֶׁן
וַיֵּאָחֲזוּ בָהּ וַיִּפְרוּ וַיִּרְבּוּ מְאֹד:

Genesis 47.27

And Israel dwelt in the land of Mitzriam, in the country of Goshen; and they had possessions in it, and grew, and multiplied exceedingly.

And He, Yisroel Dwelt
וַיֵּשֶׁב
And He, Dwelt
318 = 2ב 300ש 10י 6ו

Yisrael did not settle in or live in Mitzraim. He dwelt there. It was like he was at a stop sign with his engine running waiting for the light to turn green so he could go. Yaakov Said to Pharaoh, '...The years of my temporary residence...' Genesis 47.9

Ha Torah Says Kayin went from the Presence of The Lord and וַיֵּשֶׁב Vah Yey Shehv and dwelt. It may seem like he set up permanent residence but he did not. The Torah portion of the Hebrew Bible Says *'...You will be unsettled and a wanderer in the earth.'* Genesis 4.12.

So even though Yisroel was in Mitzriam this was only a step in his long journey to return to Eretz Canaan. Yisroel chose not to dwell on the going down, or the living there, but the coming up.

While Yisroel was staying in Mitzraim He was dwelling on what the Creator Said to Him.

Genesis 46.4
'I will go down with you to Mitzraim; and I will also surely bring you up again...'

Yisroel's focus was upon his return to Eretz Canaan.

Yaakov had very great and very powerful experiences. Yisroel had the type of experiences that we long for. Yet even though he had these marvelous experiences that were very, very powerful, they were just one night each. Yaakov's dream of a ladder extending into the gates of the Heavens was just a night. Yaakov wrestling with his brother's guardian angel was just a night. What is the point? When we experience a Spiritual Holiness such as these it is important to remember life is lived in the real world. These great experiences are intended to help us in our living and surviving in the real world.

שׁוּבִי
Shoo Vee / Return
318= 10י 2ב 6ו 300ש

Bereisheit 41.28

הוּא הַדָּבָר אֲשֶׁר **דִּבַּרְתִּי** אֶל־פַּרְעֹה אֲשֶׁר
הָאֱלֹהִים עֹשֶׂה הֶרְאָה אֶת־פַּרְעֹה׃

Genesis 41.28

This is the Word that I Spoke to Pharaoh about what God is about to do...

דִּבַּרְתִּי

Yisroel Dwelt in the Word, God Gave to Yoseif and the Word the Lord Spoke to him, *'I will go down with you to Mitzriam; and I will also surely bring you up again...'* Genesis 46.4.

Yisroel Dwelt in the Word of The Creator, '...*I will there make of you a great nation...'* Genesis 46.3.

Genesis 45.14-28

So he sent his brothers away, and they departed; and he said to them, See that you fall not out by the way. And they went up from Mitzrim, and came to the land of Canaan to Jacob their father, And told him, saying, Yoseif is yet alive, and he is governor over all the land of Mitzrim. And Yaakov's heart fainted, for he believed them not. And they told him all the words of Yoseif, which he had said to them; and when he saw the wagons which Yoseif had sent to carry him, the spirit of Yaakov their father revived; And Yisroel said, It is enough; Yoseif my son is yet alive; I will go and see him before I die.

Our Sages Teach that Yoseif shared Words from הַתּוֹרָה Ha Torah that Yisroel and He were studying before he was sold into slavery. Rabbi Avrohom Davis, The Mesudah Chumash A New Linear Translation Bereishis (Hoboken New Jersey, KTVA Publishing House, Inc., 1991) p 509

Genesis 46.2
Yisroel Dwelt in Ha Torah, '...And God spoke to Israel in the visions of the night...'

הַתּוֹרָה
Ha Torah
616 = 5ה 200ר 6ו 400ת 5ה

Genesis 47.27
And He, Israel dwelt in the land of Egypt, in the land of Goshen; and they had possessions in it, and grew, and multiplied exceedingly.

The results were Blessings:
וַיֵּאָחֲזוּ בָהּ וַיִּפְרוּ וַיִּרְבּוּ מְאֹד

45 = 5ה 2ב   6ו 7ז 8ח 1א 10י 6ו

302 = 6ו 200ר 80פ 10י 6ו

269 = 4ד 1א 40מ   6ו 2ב 200ר 10י 6ו
616 = 45 + 302 + 269

We see the Word... The Blessing and The Torah... each are the Gematria of 616. We know that when one dwells in Ha Torah and in The Words of Ha Torah they will prosper and be

Blessed regardless of the location they are temporarily at.

Vayechi

Genesis 47.28 - 50.26

This is the twelfth Parshat of twelve within the book of Genesis. Vayechi means *'and he lived'.*

Bereisheit 50.21

How Does One Comfort?

This discussion is about learning to offer comfort when the situation presents itself. One night I was in bed as a youngster with my father's beat up portable radio. I was listening to a program when all of the sudden an announcement was made of a horrible accident. As a little boy I could do nothing for those who were injured just a half dozen blocks away but my father could. I got up went to the bedroom door of my parents and knocked. One should not enter their parents bedroom without being invited. My father said something like , 'Yes son, what is it?' I informed him of the accident. My father was moved. He got out of bed dressed and drove to the scene of the accident. Three young men had died at the scene. There was little my father could do. However he did not stop there. He drove to the hospital where the parents would come to identify the bodies of their sons. He waited there to comfort each father and mother. Daddy came home around 4 am after comforting three mothers and father who lost their sons. He spoke soft words of comfort. He quoted Psalms. He prayed with them and said he was there for them if they needed him. I will always remember these kind acts. May Daddy rest in peace.

Genesis 50.14-21

And Joseph returned to Egypt, he, and his brothers, and all who went up with him to bury his father, after he had buried his father. And when Joseph's brothers saw that their father was dead, they said, Joseph will perhaps hate us, and will certainly pay us back for all the evil which we did to him. And they sent a messenger to Joseph, saying, Your father did command before he died, saying, So shall you say to Joseph,

Forgive, I beg you now, the trespass of your brothers, and their sin; for they did to you evil; and now, we beg you, forgive the trespass of the servants of the God of your father. And Joseph wept when they spoke to him. And his brothers also went and fell down before his face; and they said, Behold, we are your servants. And Joseph said to them, Fear not; for am I in the place of God? But as for you, you thought evil against me; but God meant it to good, to bring to pass, as it is this day, to save much people alive. Now therefore do not fear; I will nourish you, and your little ones. And he comforted them, with words to elevate their hearts.

Dear Ones, what we have just read is a great example of DOING WHAT IS RIGHT! Yoseif's brothers tried to alter the Prophetic Dreams that The Lord God Gave to Yoseif. The brothers were mean to Yoseif. The brothers kidnapped Yoseif. The brothers sold Yoseif into slavery. Over the course of time the circumstances changed. Through God's Blessing Yoseif shed the clothes of slavery and became a leader in Egypt. Yoseif was now powerful. Yoseif was a ruler of the most wealthy and powerful country of his time. Yoseif had authority. Yoseif had great wealth. Yoseif could have misused his great power and influence to make it difficult on his brothers yet Yoseif chose not to retaliate for what his brothers did to him. This is truly an example of Psalms 37.23

Psalm 37.23
The Steps of the Strong are Ordered by The Lord and He Delights in His Way.

Dear Ones, why do arguments escalate? It's because one does not properly employ strength. Why does one feel the need to retaliate? Why does one feel the need to 'GET EVEN'? Why does one feel the need to make another person suffer... to make them pay...

Yoseif was in a position to make his brothers pay. Yoseif could have retaliated but he didn't. Yoseif didn't escalate his brothers poor behavior, he just let it pass. We do not read of Yoseif attempting to get even. INSTEAD Yoseif took the higher road. In other Words, he was חַנּוּן Chah Noon, meaning

Gracious. The Lord God Describes Himself as חַנּוּן Chah Noon, meaning Gracious in Exodus 22.26 [KJV 27]. The Ha Torah Says that Yoseif comforted his brothers and spoke kind Words to their hearts.

The Word for Comfort is וַיְנַחֵם Vah Yih Nah Chaym. The Gematria is 114. Dear Ones, we have the same choice as Yoseif. Our Creator has Ordered us to be strong. What is it like to be strong? We can take the high road by offering comfort and being Gracious like our Creator to those who have injured us with words or deeds. We can ease mistakes by being forgiving. We can relax tense minutes by being humble... civil... well mannered... tactful... diplomatic... friendly... and amiable.

חַנּוּן
Chah Noon, / Gracious
114 = 50ן 6ו 50נ 8ח

וַיְנַחֵם
Vah Yih Nah Chaym
114 = 40ם 8ח 50נ 10י 6ו

The higher road is to give hope to those who have failed. We MUST be confident and convincing. When an individual is angry we reverse. We are not angry with them. When an individual shouts. We reverse. We speak softly. When an individual uses poor language we reverse. We use beautiful Words from Ha Torah. In other Words we Observe the Statutes, the Orders of Ha Torah. The Gematria for וְחָק Vih Chawk, meaning 'and a Stature' of Ha Torah is 114.

וְחָק
Vih Chawk, 'and a Stature' [of Ha Torah]
114 = 100ק 8ח 6ו

The way we counteract difficult issues is through Observances of Ha Torah. Only The Words of Ha Torah are Perfect. Only the Words of Ha Torah have the power to RESTORE! In My book entitled Eve Of Creation - RESTORED I share Torah Gematrias that restore us and our relationships. **CHAZAK! חזק**

GEMATRIA CHART					
Aleph	א	1			
Bet	ב	2			
Gimmel	ג	3			
Dalet	ד	4			
Hey	ה	5			
Vav	ו	6			
Zayin	ז	7			
Chet	ח	8			
Tet	ט	9			
Yud	י	10			
Chof	כ	20	Final	ך	500
Lamid	ל	30			
Mem	מ	40	Final	ם	600
Nun	נ	50	Final	ן	700
Samech	ס	60			
Ayin	ע	70			
Pey	פ	80	Final	ף	800
Tzzadi	צ	90		ץ	900
Quf	ק	100			
Reish	ר	200			
Shin	ש	300			
Tav	ת	400			

Scripture Index

Genesis	Pages	Genesis	Page
1.1 - 4	19, 20, 23	21.8 - 14	52
1.1	21	21.10	47
1.2	21	21.12	47
1.3	21	21.14	51
2.12	121	25.1	46, 53, 54
4.12	121	25.6	56
6.9	27, 28, 63	25.20	53
12.3	36	25.27	61
13.4	33, 34	28.1 - 5	65
15.1	36	28.31	93
16.2	53	29.11	76
16.3	49, 54	29.17	72
18.3 - 8	29, 30	29.18	77
18.4, 5	39, 40	29.28	93
19.3	31	29.31	93
19.27	50	29.32	94
20.1 - 18	114 - 116	29.33	94

Genesis	Page	Genesis	Page
29.34	94	46.4	122
30.21	94	47.9	121
32.4, 5	83, 84	47.27	120, 125
32.29	87	50.14 - 21	128, 129
33.29	87	50.19, 20	105
35.10	88		
37.3	93		
37.4	96		
37.5 - 11	102, 103		
37.9	103	Exodus	
37.11	96, 98, 99	1.8	44
37.18 - 20	99	12.39	31
37.20	103	21.7 - 11	54, 55
37.31	101	22.20	85
41.1	108	22.26	131
45.14 - 28	123, 124	34.23	89
46.2	124		
46.3	123		

Leviticus	Page	Proverbs	Page
19.2	86	5.18	79
19.16	86		
		Job	Page
Numbers	Page	1.3	80
19.26	110		
		Ezekiel	Page
Deut	Page	12	44
8.3	43		
29.10	51	1 Samuel	Page
34.12	15	25	76
Psalms	Page	Isaiah	Page
37.23	130	52.1	85
126.5	78, 79	52.7	41
Gemera			
Gittin - 75b		53	
Pirkei Avot - 21		5.1	
Kesuvot - 60b		53	

Gematria's			
Gematria	Page		
13	67, 68, 69	613	23, 42, 84
36	96	613	90
78	110	616	125
86	117	618	87, 90
114	131, 132	620	63
182	73	626	74
206	99	701	50
244	77	761	16
303	52	780	97
318	121, 123	845	78
395	61		
430	48		
440	64		
490	28, 32, 64		
558	42, 43, 44		
570	104		
611	35. 36		

About The Author

Dr. Akiva Gamliel Belk

Jewish, Husband, Father, Grandfather and Step Great Grandfather.

Graduate:
A.A. Long Beach City College,
B.A. Southern California Bible College,
M.A. Southern California Theological Seminary,
D. Th. Southern California Theological Seminary,
D. Th. Denver Charismatic Theological Seminary

Individual Study:
Rabbi Dovid Nusbaum,
Bais Medrash at Yeshiva Toras Chaim,
Hornosteipler Rebbe, Mordicai Tewerski
Group Study:
Rabbi Yaakov Meyer, Aish Denver
Rabbi Yisroel Engel, Director, Colorado Chabad.

Founder:
Jewishpath.org
Jewishlink.net
7commands.com
Bnti.us

Dean of Jewish Studies

B’nai Noach Torah Institute, LLC – Biblical Online Studies

Author of various books.
bnti.us/books.html

Businessman:
Realtor and Property Investor

Books By Dr. Akiva Gamliel

A Sincere Journey Ends Without Jesus
This is an autobiography of my spiritual journey. My journey did not begin with the goal of returning to Judaism. My journey began with a desire to give my Baptist Congregation a historical view of Jesus last six days on earth. My journey has been very challenging for me. If you read this book and if you walk in my footprints believing in Jesus will become a challenge for you also. The difference is I am on this side of the journey now. I have returned to Judaism. The journey of my life can be of great help to you if you discern there are problems with the story the New Testament story of Jesus.

Gematria And Mysticism IN GENESIS - Book I
Book 1 covers Genesis Chapters 1 through 10. In this series of books the reader will be introduced to truths not discussed among the religions of the world. Hebrew in the Bible unveils answers to many mysteries. The entire Bible is founded upon Genesis, Exodus, Leviticus, Numbers and Deuteronomy and the

truths that flow out of these five books is different than the rest of the Bible. Why? There is a system of Hebrew Letters with which each have a numerical value that have the power to reveal interesting and mystifying relationships within the Hebrew Letters, Words, Phrases etc. of the First Five Books. The cost of this book is a small investment for what the reader will learn.

Gematria And Mysticism IN GENESIS - Book II
Book 2 is a continues where Book 1 concluded. Book 2 covers Genesis Chapters 11 through 20.

Mysterious SIGNS Of The Torah in GENESIS
Mysterious SIGNS Of The Torah Revealed In GENESIS is an exploration of Biblical truths organized into the Weekly Parshat study of the Bible. Dr. Akiva Gamliel has been recording and referencing decades of study and research. He has gathered, compiled and organized years of discovery into this mystical book for us to learn, enjoy and share. Many years can pass between one discovery to another which forms a bridge between two discoveries. Revelations are the product of many bridges. Enclosed in this book

are some of these special relationships.

Mysterious SIGNS Of The Torah in EXODUS
This is the second in a series of Five Books, God Willing. This book is deep, intense, inspiring and extremely interesting. Yet, it is easy to read and follow. Dr. Akiva Gamliel includes a Gematria Chart in the beginning of the book . Like each of Dr. Akiva Gamliel's Gematria books there are special Gematrias waiting for the Reader to discover. There is a special sweetness in sharing a Torah Gematria / Sign during a wonderful warm Friday evening Shabbat meal or on another occasion.

Eve Of Creation RESTORED
Good people make bad mistakes. We are at times careless instead of cautious. We hurt those we love. We become angry for no apparent reason and tense without a trigger. We feel frustration! It feels like life has dealt us a loosing hand. We need a new life. We think, what would it be like to have a new life? We day dream of a place and a time that is different than where we are... We feel like we are on an endless

downward spiral. It feels like, if there were any hope, it is a great distance away... We are unhappy with our relationship... relationships... our employment... our earning capacity... our children... It's like everything around us smells!

What do we do? How do we face our endless, whatever? How do we put a stop to our seemingly endless downward spiral? The answer is simple. We repair and restore our image of Eve of Creation. Ha Torah Reveals through HOLY Numbers and Letters how to reverse improper behaviors and IMPROVE our selves.

Would You Like To Be Jewish ?

Many readers would like to know what it is like to be Jewish. Some have tried to learn what it is like to be Jewish. Some visited with a Rabbi who may have said, something like this, 'Why do you want to convert? Why do you want to be Jewish? We don't do conversions in Judaism.' You ended up walking away disappointed, angered, exasperated, annoyed and very dissatisfied. This book answers questions about what Jewish believe in a way you will not forget.

Would You Like To Be Jewish 2 ?
This is a continuation of the first book, Would You Like To Be Jewish. In this book we learn that God has always had a plan, even before the beginning of Creation. We learn how God Teaches us to repent when we fail and when we make mistakes. We discover God is very understanding, compassionate and forgiving. We share about fallen angels, , Satan, hell and how to live eternally with God.

PASSOVER –
The LAST SIX DAYS of Jesus Life On Earth
The Gospel Writers each offer a different perspective of Jesus last six days on Earth. They differ some. I offer my own perspective as a Jew that has been on both sides of this discussion. If you are a Christian... If you believe in Jesus this book will be very challenging. I started on this Journey almost 30 years ago with a desire to give my Baptist Congregation a historical view of Jesus last six days on earth. Since then I have returned to Judaism. I share some of the untold stories and fill in some of the blank pages... My journey can be of great help to you if you discern

there are problems with the story the story the Christian Writers tell of Jesus last six days on earth.

The Biblical Historical Calendar Book

The Biblical Historical Calendar Book covers many goals for all walks of life. My calender is a religious calendar and a compilation of many prized wild life photographs including trophy Mule Deer, Elk, Rocky Mountain Goats, Coyotes and Foxes and beautiful birds.

The Biblical Historical Calendar Book focuses on the History of the Bible and the beauty of nature. There is a great deal to learn about the Bible's Calendar while at the same time enjoying some breath taking wildlife photographs. This book provide the readers with interesting information about the measurement of time in the Bible and more than a dozen photographs from my prized nature and wildlife photograph collection. Doors open to many special journeys. Walk in the paths of Noah, Abraham and Moses. Learn how today's calendar is much different from the Biblical Calendar. Why the Biblical calendar changed?

How that has impacted us.

We will take an adventure with Noah on the ark. We will follow the Children of Israel out of Egypt to Mount Sinai where The Lord Gave us the Commandments. This is a book that every household can and will enjoy for years to come. This is an investment that will pay dividends the rest of your life. The Biblical Historical Calendar Book is a precious tool that offers each of us many dates of spirituality and celebration. I wish you much pleasure and enjoyment as you travel through the history of the Bible.

Order Additional Books At:

http://www.bnti.us/books.html

www.ingramcontent.com/pod-product-compliance
Lightning Source LLC
LaVergne TN
LVHW020632100826
845148LV00012B/2151

9780615952567